A TEENAGER'S A TO Z GUIDE TO EARTH SCHOOL

The Life Lessons I Wish I Knew When I Was You

Liam Mulhall

BEACON
AND
QUILL
PUBLISHING

Published in Australia in 2025 by Beacon and Quill Publishing

Text copyright © 2025 Liam Mulhall
Cover, illustrations © 2025 Liam Mulhall
Interior design by Veronica Scott

The moral rights of the author have been asserted. This book is copyrighted. Apart from any fair dealing for private study, research, criticism, or review, as permitted under the Copyright Act, no part may be reproduced or transmitted without the publisher's written permission.

All rights reserved.

Cataloguing Information

A Catalogue-in-Publication entry for this book is
available from the National Library of Australia.
A Catalogue-in-Publication entry for this book is available
from the National Library of New Zealand.
A Catalogue record for this book is available from the British Library.

United States of America Library of Congress Control Number: 2025916119
Dewey Number: 158.1

ISBN (Paperback): 978-1-76415-580-9
ISBN (Hardcover): 978-1-76415-589-2
ISBN (eBook): 978-1-76415-581-6

Printed in Australia
Designed by Liam Mulhall

10 9 8 7 6 5 4 3 2 1.

For my late mum, Patricia Walton—
I love you.
I feel you with me in every chapter of this journey.
Love you millions!!
L U B 14

And to my Aunty Nancy—
My godmother, my compass, my steady light through it all.
Thank you for guiding me with love and wisdom.

TABLE OF CONTENTS

Welcome to Earth School 1

A Acne, ADD & ADHD, Alcohol, Anxiety 5

B Bullying, Boundaries, Body Image 10

C Confidence, Consent, Comparison, Connection 13

D Depression, Discipline, Dreams 18

E Emotional Intelligence, Empathy, Experiences 22

F Fitness, Friendships, Failure, Forgiveness, Flow 26

G Gambling, Gratitude, Gender Identity, Goals 35

H Health (Mental & Physical), Habits, Heartbreak 40

I Identity, Insecurities, Integrity 45

J Jealousy, Judgment, Joy 49

K Kindness, Karma, Knowledge 53

L Love, Loyalty, Loneliness 58

M Mental Health, Materialism, Mindfulness, Money 61

N Negativity, Nudity (Online), Needs vs. Wants 68

O Overthinking, Openness, Online Life 74

P Purpose, Porn, Peer Pressure 79

Q Questions, Queerness, Quiet Time 84

R Resilience, Respect, Rest, Relationships 88

S Self-Esteem, Self-Compassion, Spirituality, Stress, Social Media 98

T	Trust, Time Management, Toxicity	106
U	Understanding, Uncertainty, Uniqueness	111
V	Virginity, Virtues, Values	116
W	Worry, Work Ethic, Worthiness	119
X	X-Factor (Your Unique Gift)	123
Y	Yes vs. No, Youth Power, You Matter	125
Z	Zest for Life, Zero Regrets, Zones (Comfort vs Growth)	128

Congratulations, Graduate of Earth School (So Far…)	132
About the Author	134

INTRODUCTION

WELCOME TO EARTH SCHOOL

No one hands you a manual when you're born. There's no guidebook for growing up, no cheat codes for figuring out who you are or how to deal with the messiness of life. But if life is a journey, consider this book your compass.

You're enrolled in what I like to call Earth School—the wildest, weirdest, most wonderful school there is. There are no clear rules, the exams come without warning, and the lessons usually show up disguised as heartbreak, hard choices, mistakes, and moments that shake you to your core.

I wrote this for you, the teenager trying to understand it all. The one who feels everything deeply, questions the world around them, and sometimes wonders if they're the only one struggling. You're not.

This book is filled with advice I wish someone had given me when I was your age. It's raw, honest, and respectful of the fact that your life matters and your choices matter. You won't find lectures here, just reflections, short stories, quotes, and real talk on everything from acne to anxiety, trust to toxic friends, and even the stuff adults get awkward about, like sex, identity, or heartbreak.

Each chapter is a letter. Each letter is a life lesson. Some will hit hard. Others will open your eyes. A few might even change your life. But most of all, they'll remind you that you're not alone.

SPECIAL ASSIGNMENTS SECTION STARTS HERE:

Some of us are here to learn how to speak up. Others are here to learn how to let go. And a few of us are here to break generational cycles that have gone unbroken for decades.

You might not realise it yet, but life constantly gives you little assignments, things to master that aren't marked by grades, stars, or certificates. These "Special Assignments" are often disguised as struggles. Like:
- Loving someone hard to love.
- Letting go of control.
- Learning to speak up when it's uncomfortable.
- Forgiving someone who never apologised.
- Trusting again after being hurt.

Sometimes, they show up early. Sometimes, they come later. But everyone has their curriculum, a unique path they're here to walk.

Let me show you what that might look like.

A SAMPLE STUDENT JOURNEY

Gabriel was the kind of student that teachers didn't quite understand. He was bright but quiet and had this invisible wall around him. At home, things weren't easy. His dad worked away. His mum was overwhelmed. Gabriel often felt like an afterthought, like he had to figure life out alone.

His Earth School curriculum wasn't chemistry or essay writing. It was learning how to express emotions he was never taught to name. It was courageously saying "I need help" without feeling weak. His "Special Assignment" was learning to believe he mattered, even when no one was clapping for him.

He's still learning and still growing. Just like the rest of us.

You are not graded. Let that land. No stars, no checklists. Just growth.

So, pick a letter, start anywhere, and take what you need.

Use this book to understand yourself better, and then maybe help others along the way. Because Earth School isn't just about learning for you. It's about growing into the kind of person who leaves this world better than they found it.

And if no one has told you this in a while: You matter. You're worthy. And I'm glad you're here.

WELCOME TO EARTH SCHOOL!

 ACNE, ADD & ADHD, ALCOHOL, ANXIETY

Story: The Mirror and the Party

Jackson stood in front of the mirror, poking at a new zit that had erupted just above his eyebrow. "Perfect," he muttered. It was Friday night, and everyone was going to a party. He'd been looking forward to it all week, but now he didn't want to show his face.

At the party, someone handed him a drink. "Come on, loosen up." Jackson hesitated. He didn't want to drink, but he didn't want to feel like *the boring one*. He sipped it. One drink turned into three. That night, he laughed, danced, and forgot about the zit. But the next morning? The anxiety hit harder than any hangover.

He realised something: you can't drink away insecurity. It's still there in the morning.

Advice & Wisdom

ACNE

It sucks, it's common, and it *does not define you*. Seriously, around 85% of teenagers deal with it. Social media filters lie. Real skin has texture, pimples, pores, and scars—and that's *normal*.

Tips:
- Don't pick at them. It makes it worse.
- Wash gently. Over-scrubbing irritates them.
- See a GP or dermatologist if it's awful. Help is out there.
- But also, your friends love your personality, not your skin.

ADD/ADHD

ADD (Attention Deficit Disorder) and ADHD (Attention Deficit Hyperactivity Disorder) show up in all sorts of ways. You might:
- Struggle to pay attention.
- Get bored easily unless it's something you love.
- Interrupt, talk a lot, or feel like your body can't sit still.
- Forget stuff, lose things, or feel like your brain's in a pinball machine.
- Or, weirdly, hyper-focus for hours on things you're passionate about.

Does this resonates with you? You're not alone. You're not flawed. A racing brain isn't a flaw, it's a superpower, if you can understand how to harness it.

Some people's minds are like steady bicycles. Others are more like race cars; fast, powerful, but harder to steer. That's ADD/ADHD.

You might learn in a different way, feel things more intensely, or take longer to get into a task than others do. That doesn't mean there's something wrong with you. It just means your brain is wired in its own unique way.

And that difference? It's not a flaw—it's a form of strength.

In the right space, with the right people who get you, those differences can actually set you apart. You might pick up on things others miss. You might see the world in more colour, connect dots in creative ways, or solve problems by thinking completely outside the box.

It's easy to feel out of place when the world rewards speed, sameness, or silence. But don't shrink to fit in. The things that make you "different" might be the very things that make you powerful.

Where does it come from?
You weren't born "wrong." No one is born with ADD/ADHD the way we think.

Dr. Gabor Maté, a world-renowned physician and trauma expert (read *Scattered Minds*), explains that ADD/ADHD can sometimes come from early childhood stress or trauma. When a child doesn't feel emotionally safe or fully connected, their brain adapts. It becomes hyper-aware, sensitive, distracted, not as a flaw, but as a survival strategy.

Other possible contributors:
- Overstimulating environments (Too much noise, chaos or pressure).
- Highly processed food or artificial additives.
- Genetic factors (like how you process folate or chemicals in your brain like dopamine).

ADD/ADHD can feel like a curse at times — especially in environments that expect you to sit still, stay silent, and stay focused for hours.
You might process things differently, feel emotions more intensely, or need more time to get into the zone. That doesn't mean there's anything wrong with you.
It just means your brain has its own rhythm and works in its own unique way, and that's okay

What can help?
You don't have to "fix" yourself. But you can learn to work with your brain, not against it.

Helpful tools include:
- A calm, structured routine — ADD/ADHD thrives in clarity, not chaos.
- Decluttering your space — seriously, a tidy room helps a busy mind.

- Movement and exercise — a proven game-changer for focus and energy.
- Mindfulness, breathwork, or grounding techniques.
- Talking to a psychologist, mentor, or trusted adult.
- Learning about how your unique brain works — so you can play to your strengths.

Quote to remember
"Your brain might be a race car. That means you must learn to drive it, not crash it." — Liam Mulhall

ALCOHOL

It might feel like a shortcut to confidence, but it's shaky. It messes your decision-making, can escalate your problems, and doesn't fill the hole you might be trying to numb.

Ask yourself:
- Why am I drinking?
- Is this good or bad for my body or brain?
- What am I trying to avoid or forget?
- Can I still have fun without it?

ANXIETY

Anxiety doesn't always show up wearing a neon sign, sometimes it's a quiet, nagging feeling you can't shake. Sometimes it's in your body before it's in your mind. Here are some common signs:
- Racing thoughts or overthinking everything.
- Feeling tense or "on edge" all the time.
- Trouble sleeping—can't shut your brain off.
- Avoiding situations because they feel too overwhelming.
- Stomach aches, headaches, or feeling sick with no apparent reason.

- Shortness of breath or feeling like your chest is tight.
- Constantly worrying about the worst-case scenario.

You're not broken. You're not weird. You're just feeling something real that deserves support, not silence. If you notice these symptoms, you're not alone, and talking to someone about them is okay.

Quote to Remember
"You're more than your skin, stronger than your fear, and worth showing up as you, your authentic self." — Liam Mulhall

Task: The Three-Day Self-Kindness Challenge

For the next three days:
- Don't pick or comment negatively on your appearance.
- Say one kind thing to yourself in the mirror.
- Say "no" to something that doesn't align with who you are.

Then reflect: how did that feel?

 BULLYING, BOUNDARIES, BODY IMAGE

Story: The Invisible Bruises

Leila smiled at school, laughed at jokes, and posted cute selfies. But the group chat messages calling her "fat" and the classmates who snapped photos of her eating at lunch didn't leave any bruises—it wasn't physical, so no one called it bullying. Yet, it hurt just the same.

Over time, she stopped eating in public. Her confidence drained, and the cruel words began to echo in her mind. The worst part? She started to believe them.

One day, she confided in a trusted teacher. For the first time, someone recognised her pain—even if the bruises couldn't be seen.

Advice & Wisdom

BULLYING

Bullying doesn't need fists to hurt. Words, exclusion, comments, and DMs leave marks, too. And sometimes the bully is your inner voice, repeating what others once said.

If you're being bullied:
- Speak up. Silence protects the bully, not you.
- Save the evidence. Screenshots matter.
- Find your safe circle. One real friend beats ten fake ones.
- You are not the problem. Their cruelty reflects their pain, not your worth.

If you've bullied someone:
- Take responsibility. If you've hurt someone, don't make excuses or blame others. Acknowledge what you did, say sorry if you can, and try to change your behaviour so it doesn't happen again.
- You are not a bad person, but you must be better.

BOUNDARIES

Boundaries are your emotional fence. They don't push people away, they protect your peace.

Examples of boundaries:
- "I'm not okay with that joke."
- "I don't want to talk about that."
- "Please don't message me after 10 PM."
- "No is a full sentence."

You teach people how to treat you by what you allow.

BODY IMAGE

The world will try to tell you that your body must look a certain way to be loved or successful. That's a lie. You don't need abs to be accepted. You don't need curves to be confident. Your body is how you move through the world, it's not what makes you worthy. Your value isn't in your weight, shape, or how you look in a photo. It's in how you treat others, how you carry yourself in day to day life and who you are on the inside.

Reminders:
- Your body keeps you alive, that alone is worth love.
- Social media is a highlight reel, not real life. People post their best moments—the smiles, the wins, the filters. What you don't see are the breakdowns, the bad days, or the stuff they're struggling

with behind the scenes. Photos can be edited. Stories can be staged. Don't compare your behind-the-scenes to someone else's highlight reel. It's not a fair fight, and it's not real. The diet culture is a billion-dollar lie, and the supplement industry is a trillion-dollar industry.
- Confidence isn't built at the gym, it's built in your head.

Quote to Remember
"You are allowed to take up space. Set the boundary. Eat the meal. Wear the outfit. Live your life." — Liam Mulhall

Task: Rewrite the Narrative
Write down three things you've believed about your body that don't serve you anymore. Then write the truth next to each one.

Example:
- "I'm not good-looking." → "I'm unique, real, and someone's dream."
- "People will judge me." → "People judge everything, I choose to be free."

Burn the old lies, like the idea that you must look a certain way to be worthy. But don't swing so far the other way that you ignore your health either. Real self-love is taking care of yourself mentally, emotionally, and physically.

Frame the new truths: Your body doesn't have to be perfect to be respected. Confidence and health can exist together. Move your body because you care about it, not because you hate it.

C CONFIDENCE, CONSENT, COMPARISON, CONNECTION

Story: The Stage and the Scroll

Tariq signed up for the school talent show. He could rap, really rap, but the moment he got on stage, his mind flooded with doubt. *What if I mess up? What if I look stupid?* Still, he performed. He stumbled once, then caught the rhythm, and the crowd clapped anyway.

Later that night, he opened Instagram. Someone posted a clip with a comment: "Cringe." He almost deleted his account. But then he remembered: he did something brave. The critic didn't even step on stage.

Advice & Wisdom

CONFIDENCE

Confidence isn't loud. It's not cocky. It's quiet courage, the voice that says, "I'll try anyway."

Build it by:
- Keeping promises to yourself.
- Doing hard things on purpose.
- Practicing, even when no one cares.
- Speaking kindly to yourself, especially when you mess up.

Confidence isn't the absence of fear; it's the decision to act anyway.

CONSENT

Consent isn't just about sex. It's about respecting someone's body, space, choices, and boundaries, and expecting the same in return.

Real consent is:
- Freely given—not forced, pressured, or guilted.
- Reversible—anyone can change their mind at any time.
- Informed—both people understand what they're agreeing to.
- Enthusiastic—a clear yes, not just the absence of a no.
- Specific—saying yes to one thing doesn't mean yes to everything.

In practice, consent sounds like:
- "Are you okay with this?"
- "Do you want to keep going?"
- "We can stop anytime."

It should never feel one-sided or uncertain. If someone is drunk, high, afraid, confused, or hesitant, it's not consent.

In relationships and situations of any kind:
- Always ask.
- Respect "no," even if it's sudden or unexpected.
- Don't push. Don't guilt. Don't beg. That's not romance, it's control.

And remember: your boundaries deserve to be respected just as much as anyone else's.

COMPARISON

It's normal to look at others and wonder if you're enough. But comparison kills confidence. You're not supposed to be *them*. You're supposed to be *you*.

Try this instead:
- Turn jealousy into curiosity: "What does this show me about what I want?"
- Celebrate others without shrinking yourself.
- Limit your scrolling. Social media is curated, not candid.

Remember: no one posts their breakdowns, only their highlights.

Quotes to Remember
"Confidence is being yourself without apology. Consent is love in action."
— Liam Mulhall

One other favourite quote of mine is "Comparison is the thief of joy" — Theodore Roosevelt

Task: Mirror Challenge + Consent Journal

Part 1—Mirror Talk:
Look in the mirror and say three things you like about who you are—not what you look like, but who you are.

Part 2—Consent Check-In:
Think of a recent situation where you didn't feel entirely comfortable. Did you feel pressured to say yes when you wanted to say no? Or did you pressure someone else?

Write it out. Get your thoughts out of your mind and onto paper—no filters, no holding back. Then step back and reflect. This isn't about judging yourself or feeling ashamed. It's about becoming more aware of what's really going on inside you. That's how real growth begins, with honesty and self-awareness.

CONNECTION

It's not about being popular. It's about being known. It's that one mate who checks in when you go quiet. The person you can be weird with, honest with, and sad around. Connection is the glue that holds us together when life tries to pull us apart.

Having a tribe is more important than having followers!

In his book *Tribe*, war reporter Sebastian Junger says people often feel more connected during war or disasters than in everyday life. Why? Because they've got a crew. Everyone's in it together, no pretending, no fake smiles. Same vibe as when your team's down by ten, five minutes to go, and you're all digging deep—that's having a tribe.

On the flip side, Johann Hari reckons a lot of anxiety and depression today comes from disconnection. Not just from people, but from purpose, nature, and meaning. His book *Lost Connections* says we've lost everything that makes life feel real.

So maybe the fix isn't more scrolling or pretending we're fine—maybe it's finding our people, doing things that matter, and it means checking in, lending a hand, showing you care, especially when it's inconvenient.

Signs of a healthy connection:
- You feel safe being real.
- You don't have to fake it.
- You're supported, even when you're not "on."
- You laugh more. You stress less.
- You leave feeling lighter.

So, ask yourself: Who makes you feel seen? Who drains your energy? Connection should give you power, not take it away.

You don't need a hundred people. You need a few good ones—your tribe.

Connection isn't about how many people know your name, it's about who knows your silence. It's not about who claps the loudest when you win, but who notices when your energy fades, when your messages change, or when you stop showing up. True connection lives in the quiet moments, in the check-ins that don't ask for anything in return, in the "just thinking of you" texts when you haven't said a word.

Your tribe isn't loud, it's loyal. It doesn't need to be big. In fact, most of the time, it's small. It's the friend who sees through your fake smile, the one who hears the heaviness in your "I'm fine," and sits with you anyway. They don't need constant updates, they just *know* when something's off.

They're not followers. They're the ones who stay when you fall quiet. In a world obsessed with attention, it's easy to mistake being seen for being known. But real connection is quieter than that. It shows up in consistency, not clout. It's not about popularity, it's about presence.

If you have even one person who sees the real you, the unfiltered, messy, unspoken parts, you're already rich in ways the world can't measure.

Quote to Remember
"Connection isn't just being around people. It's about feeling seen and heard for who you really are." —Hailey Hardcastle

D DEPRESSION, DISCIPLINE, DREAMS

Story: The Mask and the Matchstick

Ellie was the funny one who always had a comeback and laughed the loudest. But when she got home, the silence hit like a wall. Her motivation vanished, her room got darker, and her texts went unanswered.

One day, her friend noticed. "You're not okay, are you?" Ellie didn't cry. She just nodded. That moment, that *one* question, lit a match in the dark. It didn't fix everything. But it started something. And that's often all it takes: one honest moment.

Advice & Wisdom

DEPRESSION

Depression doesn't always look like someone curled up in bed crying. Sometimes it's smiling in public and breaking down in private. Sometimes it feels like… nothing at all. A heavy, empty fog you can't shake.

Here are some common signs of depression:
- Feeling hopeless or emotionally numb most days.
- Losing interest in things you used to enjoy.
- Changes in sleep—sleeping too much or barely at all.
- Changes in appetite—eating more than usual or barely at all.
- Constant exhaustion, even after resting.

- Withdrawing from friends, family, or school.
- Feeling like a burden or believing the world would be better without you.

Some people may even have thoughts of hurting themselves or ending their life. If that's you, please know this: You might feel completely alone right now, like no one understands, no one would care if you disappeared, and no one could possibly help. That feeling is unbearably heavy... and it lies.

Depression wants you to believe you're the only one going through this. That you're broken, unlovable, or beyond help. But you're not. You're a human being in pain and you don't have to face it alone. There are people who care, even if you can't feel that care right now.

There are professionals trained to help. There are friends and family who may not have the right words, but who *would* drop everything if they knew how much you were hurting.

Please, reach out. Tell someone how you're feeling. Text a friend. Call a helpline. Speak to a school counsellor.

You don't have to fix everything overnight, you need to take *one* small step. Even if it's simply saying, "I don't want to be here, I want to end my life, and I don't know what to do."

That's enough. That's brave. And that's how healing begins.

If you're in Australia:
Call Lifeline on 13 11 14 or Kids Helpline on 1800 55 1800. Both are open 24/7. No judgment, just people who care.

If you're reading this elsewhere:
Search for your country's local mental health crisis line. Help is closer than you think.

You matter. You're not too much. You're not alone.

Optional Reading:
It's OK That You're Not OK by Megan Devine.

If you've ever felt like no one understands how deep your sadness runs, this book might help. It won't give you fake positivity or quick fixes, just truth: Some pain can't be "fixed." But you can learn to carry it and live through it.

You don't have to read it now. But if you ever need a quiet companion who *gets it*, this book might be there when no one else is.

DISCIPLINE

Discipline isn't punishment—it's *freedom*. It's doing what needs to be done, *especially* when you don't feel like it, because you know your future self will thank you. The things you do everyday shape who you become.
- Want confidence? Prove to yourself you can follow through.
- Want strength? Train, even when you don't feel like it.
- Want respect? Do what you say you'll do.
- Want peace? Stick to your values, even when it's not easy.

You won't rise to your goals. You'll fall to your habits. So, build good ones.

"Watch your actions, they become your habits, watch your habits, they become your character." —Vince Lombardi

DREAMS

Not just what you do at night—your *vision* for life. The stuff that makes your heart race, your mind wander, and your eyes light up. But dreams take action.

- Write them down.
- Break them into steps.
- Tell someone who will support you.
- Believe in them *before* the world does.

If your dream feels crazy, good. The best ones always do.

Quote to Remember
"Your darkness doesn't define you. Your discipline refines you. And your dreams? They're waiting—but only if you start moving." — Liam Mulhall

Task: Light in the Dark

1. Depression Check:
Write down three emotions you've felt this week. Name them. Accept them. No judgment. Then write one kind thing you'd say to a friend feeling that way. Say it to yourself.

2. Discipline Habit:
Pick one positive or productive thing, a two-minute task, and do it *every day* for the next seven days. Examples: Make your bed, go for a walk, drink water first thing in the morning, or write a journal entry. Tiny wins create massive momentum.

3. Dream Vision:
Close your eyes. Picture the life you want. Now write five things you'd be doing in that life. That's your dream's blueprint.

E EMOTIONAL INTELLIGENCE, EMPATHY, EXPERIENCES

Story: The Snap That Snapped

Josh lost it in class. A small joke, one he might've laughed at last week, suddenly made him explode. He slammed his chair back, fists clenched and stormed out.

But instead of getting detention, his teacher just found him sitting alone after class. She didn't raise her voice. She just said quietly, "That felt like more than just a joke, hey?"

Josh didn't answer. He wasn't sure how. Later that night, still chewing on the moment, he came across a quote online: "Emotional intelligence is knowing what you're feeling before your feelings take over."

And for the first time, he stopped to think. It wasn't the joke. It was everything he'd been bottling up.

Advice & Wisdom

EMOTIONAL INTELLIGENCE (EQ)

Your IQ might get you a job, but your EQ will keep your friendships, relationships, and peace of mind.

Emotional Intelligence starts with something simple, but not always easy: "What am I feeling right now?"

It's hard to deal with your emotions if you don't even know what they are. Emotional Intelligence isn't about solving everything. It's about paying attention to what you're feeling, even when it's messy inside.

Try this, ask yourself:
- Am I sad, or am I just tired?
- Am I angry, or am I feeling hurt?
- Am I anxious, or am I scared of not being enough?

Tip:
Give your feelings names. When you name them, they lose some of their power.

The Four Pillars of EQ:
- Self-awareness—recognising your emotions without judging them.
- Self-regulation—managing your emotions in a healthy way.
- Empathy—understanding how someone else feels.
- Social skills—communicating, listening, and connecting well with others.

Why does EQ matter?
Because feelings drive actions. And if you don't understand your feelings, they'll end up running the show—guiding your actions, your words, even your decisions—without you even realising it.

Ever said something in anger that you didn't really mean? Or shut down completely when you needed help? That's what happens when emotions take the wheel and you're not in the driver's seat.

Emotional intelligence helps you slow down and ask, "What am I actually feeling right now?" That one question gives you space to choose how you respond, instead of just reacting.

Because when you don't name your feelings, they find other ways to speak, through silence, sarcasm, outbursts, or shutdowns. And often, they don't say what you really want to express.

Having emotional intelligence doesn't mean you never feel upset or angry. It means you don't let those feelings run your life like an out-of-control bus with no driver.

EMPATHY

Empathy means being able to understand and share what someone else is feeling.

It's not about feeling sorry for them or rushing to give advice. It's about being present and letting them know they're not alone in what they're going through.

You don't need to have the perfect words. Often, just listening without judgment is enough.

Try this:

When a friend opens up, pause and listen fully—don't jump in to fix things right away.

Remind yourself that most people are trying their best, even when they fall short.

If you're feeling misunderstood, ask yourself: "Am I making the same effort to understand others"

EXPERIENCES

Everything is a teacher, even the stuff that sucks. A breakup? Teaches resilience. A mistake? Teaches humility. A win? Teaches gratitude.

Reframe it:
Not "Why is this happening to me?" But: "What can this teach me?"

Quote to Remember

"Emotional intelligence turns pain into power, empathy into connection, and experience into wisdom." — Liam Mulhall

Task: The Three Es of Reflection

1. EQ Moment:
Think of a time you overreacted. What was going on underneath?

2. Empathy Act:
Reach out to someone you know who is struggling. Ask how they're doing and listen, sit in the mud with them.

3. Experience Audit:
Write down three hard things you've gone through. Now, next to each one, write what it *taught* you.

F FITNESS, FRIENDSHIPS, FAILURE, FORGIVENESS, FLOW

Story: The Fall That Lifted Me

Luca joined the school gym with big plans: get shredded, impress his crush, and feel more confident. He went every day for two weeks, pushing hard and chasing the version of himself he wanted to become. Then he pulled something in his back and had to stop. His first instinct? To quit. What was the point if he couldn't even lift?

But he didn't quit.

He swapped the dumbbells for daily walks. He learned to stretch properly and started reading about rest and recovery. Slowly, his focus shifted. It wasn't about having abs or turning heads anymore—it was about showing up for himself. About feeling strong inside, not just looking it on the outside.

The setback humbled him. It made him slow down, listen to his body, and build real discipline.

He found himself in the fall.

Not in the mirror, or the PRs, or the attention—but in the quiet moments of starting again. In choosing growth over ego. That's when he began to understand what real strength actually looks like.

Advice & Wisdom

FITNESS

It's not about abs. It's about energy. Discipline. Confidence. It's about feeling strong in your own skin—whatever that looks like.

Fitness isn't just about what you see in the mirror. It's about what you feel in your mind, in your mood, in your ability to take on the day. A regular movement routine, whether that's walking, lifting, swimming, dancing, or just kicking a ball around can help you clear your head, boost your energy, and feel more in control when everything else feels a bit too much.

There's so much pressure to chase the "perfect" body, especially online. But here's the truth: Working out isn't payback for eating. It's proof your body is strong and worth looking after.

And the goal isn't perfection. It's progress. Showing up, even when you don't feel like it. Moving your body in a way that feels good and sustainable. That's the kind of strength that lasts.

Fitness truths to live by:
- Start small. A fifteen-minute walk is better than nothing. Consistency beats intensity every time.
- You don't have to love the gym. Find what moves *you*, whether it's dancing, hiking, team sports, or skating.
- Fuel your body. Eat to nourish, not to punish.
- Move to feel better, not to shrink yourself.
- Fitness isn't just about building muscle. It builds *resilience*. It teaches you to keep going when things get hard. That's where the growth is.

Think of fitness as self-respect in motion. You're not just shaping your body, you're shaping your habits, your mindset, and your relationship with yourself.

FRIENDSHIPS

Good friends grow with you. Fake ones drain you.

You become like the people you hang around—so choose them like your future depends on it. Because honestly, it kind of does.

Friendships in your teen years shape more than your social life—they shape your confidence, your choices, your standards, and even your sense of self. The right people will help you rise. The wrong ones will pull you into things that don't feel right, just to keep you close.

You don't need a hundred friends. You don't even need ten. You need *one or two real ones* who get you, challenge you kindly, and have your back—without making you question your worth.

Healthy friendships feel like:
- Safe spaces, not minefields—where you don't have to filter your personality or walk on eggshells.
- Supportive, not jealous—cheering each other on without turning everything into a competition.
- Honest, not judgmental—able to tell you the truth, even when it's uncomfortable, because they care.
- Respectful of your boundaries, goals, and changes—even if they don't fully understand them yet.

It's important to know: a real friend won't just tell you what you want to hear, they'll tell you what you need to hear. That's not being mean. That's being loyal in the truest sense.

Being supportive doesn't mean being sycophantic. If someone agrees with everything you do just to stay liked, that's not love—it's fear in disguise. Real friends care more about you than your approval.

And you owe the same in return. Be the kind of friend who lifts others, not one who pressures them to shrink to make you feel bigger. Friendship is a mirror—what you give tends to reflect.

Choose people who make you feel seen, not just surrounded. It's better to walk alone than follow the crowd in the wrong direction.

FAILURE

Failure isn't the opposite of success; it's the path to it. Every person you admire—athletes, artists, inventors, leaders—has failed more times than you can count. What separates them from the rest isn't luck. It's that they kept showing up.

Let's redefine failure: Fail = First Attempt In Learning.

You didn't fail. You just found a way that didn't work—yet. Like learning to ride a bike, you wobble, fall, and maybe scrape your knee. But each attempt teaches you something. That's how growth works. Nobody nails it on their first go—not the musicians you listen to, the athletes you cheer for, or the entrepreneurs you admire. They all learned by failing, adjusting, and trying again.

Fall forward. When you fall, fall with purpose. Learn from it. Move an inch closer to where you want to be. Falling forward means you're not going back into fear or self-doubt—you're using the fall as momentum. Every mistake brings you new insight, new grit, and new strength. That's how champions are made.

You're not starting from scratch, you're starting from experience. After failure, you carry something you didn't have before: Wisdom.

Experience. Clarity. You're better equipped than the first time. Think of it like levelling up in a game—you might get knocked out, but you respawn smarter. Every setback plants the seeds for your comeback.

Here's the truth: Every single person who's ever done something worthwhile has failed. Repeatedly. Loudly. Privately. Publicly. It's not something to fear—it's something to expect, embrace, and grow from.

When faced with adversity, a proactive response that involves learning from mistakes is superior to freezing or fleeing. Because you're not failing at life. You're learning how to live it.

Quote to Remember

"Failure meant a stripping away of the inessential... Rock bottom became the solid foundation on which I rebuilt my life." — J. K. Rowling

Task: Friendship Check, Failure Reflection & Fitness Goal

1. Friendship Check: Who's in Your Corner?
List of your five closest friends. Now ask yourself—not in anger or frustration, but with honesty and empathy:
- Do they *listen* when you say no or need space?
- Do they *celebrate* when good things happen to you, or do they change the subject?
- Do they make you feel like you can be your full, authentic self, even on bad days?

No friend is perfect. Just like you, they're still learning how to show up, how to care, how to communicate. So don't rush to cut people off because of one fight or misunderstanding.

Instead, look for patterns:
- Do they *usually* lift you up, or often pull you down?

- Do they *own up* when they mess up, or always blame someone else?
- Are you growing better around them or shrinking?

If someone keeps crossing your boundaries, putting you down, or making you feel like you must earn their approval, it's okay to take a step back. You're not being mean. You're just protecting your peace.

Empathy works both ways. Be kind—but be clear about what you deserve.

2. Fitness Goal: Move, Even If You Mess Up

Choose one simple ten-minute movement habit and do it three times this week. You can walk, stretch, kick a footy, dance in your room, anything that gets your body moving.

But here's the twist: If you miss a day, or even all three, you haven't failed, you've learned what gets in your way.

Ask:
- Was I tired? Unmotivated? Distracted?
- What can I try next week that might work better?

Failure isn't the end, it's a teacher. It's how you figure out what doesn't work so you can move closer to what does.

3. Failure Reflection: What Did It Teach You?

You can't plan for failure, but you *can* learn from it. Think back to something that didn't go the way you hoped:
- A bad grade.
- A falling out with someone.
- A time you let yourself down.

Now ask:
- What happened?
- How did I react?
- What did I learn?
- What would I do differently next time?

You're not the only one who's ever failed. Every person you admire has failed, probably more than you think. What sets them apart is that they didn't stop there. They fell, they reflected, they recalibrated.

So, here's your task:
Write down one thing that felt like a failure, and underneath it, write: "This wasn't the end. It was a lesson in disguise."

Then—breathe. You're not behind. You're becoming.

FORGIVENESS

Forgiveness isn't about pretending it didn't hurt. It's not about saying what they did was okay. It's about freeing yourself, so you don't carry its weight anymore.

Sometimes we wait for an apology that may never come. That doesn't mean you have to hold on to the pain. Forgiveness is something you give yourself, not the other person.

So, what does forgiveness look like?
- It looks like breathing out what you've been holding in.
- It looks like saying, "I won't let this define me anymore."
- It looks like setting boundaries, not building walls.

Who do you need to forgive?
- Maybe it's a friend who hurt you.
- Maybe it's a parent who wasn't what you needed.
- Maybe it's yourself.

Yes, forgiving yourself is part of it too, for the choices you regret, the things you didn't know, and the times you were just trying to survive.

Forgiveness is how you lighten your emotional load. Holding onto anger, shame, or regret doesn't make you stronger, it just makes the journey harder.

Letting go doesn't mean forgetting. It means *choosing yourself* over the weight of what was. You don't have to carry it anymore.

Quote to Remember
"Holding onto anger is like drinking poison and expecting the other person to die." —Gautama Buddha

FLOW

Flow, or as some people call it, the *flow state*, is that feeling when you're fully immersed in something. You lose track of time doing what you love. It could be drawing, playing footy, surfing, coding, making music, cooking, or gaming. It's the sweet spot between being challenged and being capable. You're not bored. You're not stressed. You're just *there*.

Why does flow matter? Because flow helps:
- Clear your mind.
- Boost your mood.
- Build confidence.
- Show you who you are when no one's watching.

You don't always have to be productive. But you do need to feel *present*. Flow gives you a break from overthinking. It helps you escape, not from life, but *into* something that lights you up.

Try this:
- Think of a time when hours flew by. What were you doing?
- Was your brain calm or chaotic?
- That's a clue to your flow.

Quote to Remember

"When you're in the zone, time melts. Worries fade. You're not forcing it—you're just in *it. That's flow." — Liam Mulhall*

G GAMBLING, GRATITUDE, GENDER IDENTITY, GOALS

Story: The Bet That Cost More Than Money

Kai downloaded a betting app "just for fun." At first, it was just a few small wins, nothing serious. But soon, he started chasing that feeling. Late nights. Secret losses. He stopped replying to mates, skipped hangouts, and even took money from his brother's wallet.

When it all caught up with him, Kai realised it was never really about the money. It was about the emptiness he didn't know how to talk about. The boredom. The stress. The low days that felt too hard to sit with. Gambling gave him a way to escape, a fake high to numb the lows. It filled the silence. Made him feel like he was in control, even when everything else felt out of reach.

Advice & Wisdom

GAMBLING

Gambling is often sold as harmless fun—a flutter on the pokies, a casual punt on the races, a bit of excitement during the game. But behind the flashing lights and winning jingles is a system carefully designed to keep you hooked. If you've found yourself caught in the cycle, it doesn't mean you're weak, it means you've been drawn into something that preys on hope, emotion, and distraction.

Here are some signs to watch out for:
- You gamble to escape boredom, sadness, or stress.
- You hide your losses, debts, or how often you play.
- You believe your next win will fix everything.
- You feel restless, anxious, or irritable when you're not gambling.

If any of this sounds familiar, you're not alone—and you're not broken. You deserve support, not shame. Talking to someone is a powerful first step. Shame shrinks when it's brought into the light.

Gamblers Help Line: 1800 858 858. Free. Confidential. 24/7.

Optional Reading:
One Day at a Time by Justin Rees-Larcombe.

This book isn't for everyone, but if you or someone close to you is struggling with addiction, especially gambling, it's one of the most real, practical guides out there.

Justin lost nearly everything—his family, money, and sense of self. But he turned his life around through honesty, faith, and small steps forward.

If you ever feel trapped in a habit you can't shake, this book might help you find a way out.

GRATITUDE

Gratitude isn't about pretending everything's perfect. It's about noticing the good that's already here, even when life feels messy. It won't solve your problems, but it *can* shift your focus.

Real gratitude often begins when you realise this: you don't need everything to be happy. You just need *enough*—enough love, enough food, enough support, enough peace. And chances are, you already have more than you think.

Try this:
- Write down three things you're grateful for each day, even if they're small.
- Tell someone what you appreciate about them.
- Notice the little things: a hot shower, a laugh with a mate, sunlight on your skin.

Gratitude isn't about having more. It's about realising you already have enough.

GENDER IDENTITY

Who you are, how you feel inside and how you express yourself, matters.

You deserve:
- To explore your identity safely.
- To be respected in your pronouns and presentation.
- To take your time figuring it out.

If someone comes out to you:
- Believe them.
- Respect them.
- Support them, even if you don't fully understand.

Quote to Remember
"Addiction numbs pain. Gratitude can heal it. And whoever you are—your identity is valid and deserves respect." — Liam Mulhall

Task: Gamble-Free Day & Gratitude Tracker

1. Go 24 Hours Without a Bet:

Notice the urges. What feelings come up? Replace the habit—go for a walk, talk to someone, journal.

2. Gratitude Tracker:
Write one thing every morning and night you're grateful for. Stick with it for seven days. It will rewire your brain.

GOALS

Goals don't have to be huge. You don't need to figure out your whole future by lunch. But setting goals, even small ones, gives your life direction. They're like road signs. They help you stay focused when everything feels messy or pointless.

Not every goal has to be about marks or muscles. Some real goals might look like:
- I want to feel confident speaking up in class.
- I want to wake up early and not hate it.
- I want to save a hundred dollars and not blow it on snacks.
- I want to finish this term proud of myself, not burnt out.

Quick goal tip; make your goals SMART:
- Specific.
- Measurable.
- Achievable.
- Realistic.
- Time-bound.

Example: "I want to run three times a week for thirty minutes" is better than "I want to get fit."

Be the master of your dreams. In his book *Can't Hurt Me*, David Goggins says most people let their dreams become their masters. They talk about becoming a doctor, a singer, or an athlete… but do nothing about it. It just floats there, a "one-day" fantasy.

But when you flip the script, when you become the master of your dreams, everything changes. You stop dreaming and start planning. You write a list. You map out the steps. You get uncomfortable, work hard, and keep working on it. That's how dreams become real.

So, dream big—but back it up with action. Because dreams don't work unless you do.

Small wins matter! Don't underestimate the power of ticking something off. It builds confidence, discipline, and belief.

Quote to Remember
"A goal without a plan is just a wish." —Antoine de Saint-Exupery

H HEALTH (MENTAL & PHYSICAL), HABITS, HEARTBREAK

Story: The Heart That Healed

Amira was in love. First love. Deep, intoxicating, butterflies-in-your-stomach love. Until the day it ended with a short text and a cold silence.

She couldn't eat. Couldn't sleep. Her heart physically ached. She didn't realise heartbreak could feel like actual illness.

She cried—a lot. Some days, the tears came out of nowhere. Other days, they didn't come at all, just a heavy, empty feeling in her chest. That's the thing about heartbreak—it's real grief. And grief takes time.

But she committed to one simple daily routine: drink water, stretch, and go for a walk. The ache didn't disappear, but little by little, it softened. In time, she found her footing again, and with it, a quiet strength she hadn't known she had.

Heartbreak hurts, but it's not forever. Your person *will* come, but first, focus on becoming the best version of *you*. The right person won't complete you. They'll meet you where you already feel whole.

Advice & Wisdom

HEALTH – MENTAL & PHYSICAL

One affects the other. Ignore one, and the other suffers.

- Move daily—even a little.
- Fuel your body—eat more colours, not more calories.
- Rest—sleep is your reset button.
- Protect your mental peace—it's just as vital as food or water.

Mental peace means being able to breathe without feeling like the world is crushing you. It's the ability to think clearly, sleep at night, and feel safe in your own head.

Protecting that peace doesn't always mean running away from problems — but it *does* mean setting boundaries. And sometimes, it means making hard choices:
- If a friend constantly puts you down, pressures you, or drains your energy — it's okay to step back. You're allowed to outgrow people.
- If your social media feed makes you feel like you're never enough — unfollow, mute, or log out. Your worth isn't tied to likes or views.
- If your family dynamic is toxic, and you can't escape it yet — create small pockets of peace. A walk. A journal. A playlist. A space that's yours.
- If school or a job is damaging your wellbeing — talk to someone. A teacher, a counsellor, a trusted adult. You don't have to suffer in silence.

Mental peace isn't about avoiding all discomfort — it's about not letting chaos live rent-free in your head.

You don't owe your energy to people or places that constantly take more than they give.

You matter too — and protecting your peace is one of the most powerful forms of self-respect.

HABITS

You are what you do over and over again.

It's not your big goals or best intentions that shape who you are, it's your small, everyday actions. You could have the best plan in the world, but if you never act on it, nothing changes.

But small actions? They build momentum. They create habits. And over time, they shape your identity.

So don't wait for the perfect moment. Just start, even if it's slow. Progress beats perfection every time.

Build better habits by:

- Stacking them.

Link a new habit to something you already do. For example: After I brush my teeth, I'll do thirty seconds of stretching. After I wake up, I'll make my bed right away. This makes the habit easier to remember and more automatic.

- Making them obvious, easy, and satisfying.

If you want to drink more water, leave a full bottle on your desk or by your bed. Want to read more? Keep a book where you usually scroll your phone. Start small—one page, one stretch, one glass—and celebrate it.

- Forgiving yourself when you slip, then getting back on track.

Missing one day doesn't mean you've failed. Everyone slips up. What matters is that you reset and try again the next day. Progress isn't perfect, it's consistent effort over time.

HEARTBREAK

Heartbreak can feel like your world is falling apart, like the ache might never leave. But even though it hurts deeply, it won't break you. It teaches you things no classroom ever will: what you truly value in a relationship, what kind of love feels safe and real, and what you'll never settle for again.

In the early days, it's normal to want to fill the gap, to distract yourself, jump into something new, or numb the pain. But real healing happens when you *don't* rush. When you let yourself feel it. Cry if you need to. Write. Walk. Talk to someone you trust. Give yourself time to figure out what this experience is teaching you about yourself.

Heartbreak isn't just about losing someone else—it's also a chance to find your way back to *you*. Bit by bit, you rebuild. And along the way, you grow into someone wiser, stronger, and more ready for the love you *do* deserve.

If you're struggling with heartbreak or trying to make sense of love, I recommend checking out these two books. They won't fix everything, but they might help you understand yourself better and help you find the person who gets you and all your quirks. *The Five Love Languages* by Gary Chapman and *Attached* by Dr Amir Levine and Rachel Heller.

Quote to Remember
"Heartbreak doesn't mean you were foolish for caring — it means you were brave enough to love fully. And that kind of courage? It always leaves a mark, but it also builds a stronger heart." — Liam Mulhall

Task: Habit Builder & Heart Healer

1. Build One Habit
Pick one simple, healthy habit to stick with for the next five days. It can be anything small that helps you feel better mentally, emotionally, or physically.

Examples:
- Drink a full glass of water first thing in the morning.
- Make your bed every day.

- Write down one thing you're grateful for before bed.
- Go for a ten-minute walk after school.

Track your consistency. Use a notebook, an app, or even a sticky note. The goal isn't perfection, it is being accountable, five days in a row. That's how routines begin.

2. Write a Letter to Your Heart

This isn't a letter to another person, it's a letter *to yourself*. What does your heart need to hear right now?

Maybe it's:
- A goodbye to someone you're still holding on to.
- An apology for the way you've treated yourself.
- A reminder that you're stronger than you feel.
- Or encouragement to keep going, even when it's tough.

You don't need to show anyone. You don't even have to keep it. The point is to get the emotions out of your head and onto the page. Writing can be a powerful way to start healing.

IDENTITY, INSECURITIES, INTEGRITY

Story: The Mask I Wore

Mason was the "funny guy." Always making people laugh, always turning everything into a joke. But behind the smiles, he wasn't sure who he really was without the funny act.

He used humour to cover up what he was feeling. Underneath all the jokes was fear—fear that he wasn't good enough, that if he stopped being the clown, people wouldn't like the real him.

It wasn't until he started speaking honestly—no jokes, no pretending—that things began to change. His voice was shaky at first. But it was real. And for the first time, *he* felt real too.

If you're the "funny one," that's okay. Making people laugh is a gift. But if you're always hiding behind jokes because you're scared to show what's really going on, then it's time to check in with yourself.

You don't have to be "on" all the time. You're allowed to be serious, sad, unsure, or vulnerable. The people who care about you will still be there when the jokes stop, and the right ones will care even more when they hear the real you.

Being honest isn't weakness. It's strength without the mask.

Advice & Wisdom

IDENTITY

Who you are isn't something you have to figure out all at once. It's not a fixed label, a box to tick, or something other people get to decide for you. It's a journey—and it's *yours*.

You're allowed to grow. You're allowed to change. You're allowed to explore what feels true for you today, even if it's different from yesterday.

You are not your mistakes. You're not just your past. And you're definitely not the version of yourself others expect you to be. What matters is who you're becoming, and that takes time, curiosity, and self-respect.

You don't need to have it all figured out. You just need to keep showing up for yourself, with honesty and kindness.

INSECURITIES

Everyone has them, even the people who seem confident, popular, or "put together." The truth is, most people are carrying around quiet doubts about themselves. Maybe it's their body, their voice, their background, their skin, their grades, their personality—whatever it is, it feels like something they need to hide.

But the first step in dealing with insecurity is *not* pretending it doesn't exist. Hiding it gives it more power. Saying it out loud, even just to yourself, can take away some of its weight.

Then ask: "Who told me this was a flaw?" Sometimes what we see as a weakness was only ever someone else's opinion, a cruel comment, or an unfair comparison.

And what if it's not a flaw at all? What if it's your strength in disguise? Maybe you're quiet, but that means you listen deeply and think carefully. Maybe you're sensitive, which means you feel deeply and care about others. Maybe you don't fit in, which means you're original and unafraid to be different.

The things that make you feel "less than" might be the things that make you powerful once you start owning them.

INTEGRITY

Doing the right thing, especially when no one's watching, is what integrity is all about. It's easy to act kind, respectful, or responsible when others are around. But who are you when it's just *you*?

Integrity means your actions match your values. It's picking up rubbish even if it's not yours. It's speaking up when someone's being treated unfairly even if it's uncomfortable. It's not laughing at a joke that crosses the line even if everyone else is.

Why it matters:
- It builds trust. When people know you do what's right, not just what's popular, they respect you more. And more importantly, *you* respect yourself more.
- It protects your reputation. Character is built over time, but it can fall apart fast. Integrity keeps it strong.
- It gives you peace. There's something powerful about knowing you stayed true to yourself, even when no one noticed.

You won't always get it perfect. But integrity is a muscle—the more you use it, the stronger it gets.

Quote to Remember
"In a world full of filters, being real is a radical act of courage." — Liam Mulhall

Task: Identity Reflection & Integrity Challenge

1. Who Am I?
Write ten "I am" statements. Example:
- I am creative.
- I am still healing.
- I am stronger than I look.

2. Integrity Challenge:
Do something kind without telling anyone, like sending a message, helping with a chore, or doing a favour. Not for likes or credit, just because it's the right thing to do.

You are who you are when no one's watching. And that version of you? That's the one that really matters.

J JEALOUSY, JUDGMENT, JOY

Story: The Green-Eyed Scroll

Mia couldn't stop looking at Sam's Instagram: perfect hair, friends, and boyfriend. Every scroll made Mia feel smaller, uglier, lonelier. She wasn't proud of it, but she was jealous.

Then, one day, she saw Sam crying behind the school gym. Alone, without a filter, no likes, just a real girl, hurting. Mia realized that we're all fighting battles we don't post about.

Advice & Wisdom

JEALOUSY

Jealousy isn't something to be embarrassed about, it's a *clue*. It shows you what you care about, what you wish you had, or what matters deeply to you. Instead of judging yourself for feeling it, try asking: What is this feeling trying to tell me?

When jealousy shows up, don't ignore it, and don't let it take over, either. Instead, pause and ask yourself, "What is this feeling trying to tell me?" Maybe you're jealous of someone's success, their relationship, or the attention they're getting. That's not a sign that you're mean or broken, it's a sign that *you care*. It's showing you something you wish you had, something that matters to you.

Instead of letting that feeling turn into comparison or self-doubt, turn it into curiosity. What can you learn from it? What's one small step you can take toward that thing you want, whether it's confidence, connection, recognition, or growth?

Jealousy can pull you down *or* push you forward. The choice is yours. Let it motivate you, not destroy you.

JUDGMENT

It's easy to judge someone—how they look, what they wear, how they act, or who they hang out with. But before you do, pause and remind yourself: you're only seeing a snapshot.

You don't see what's going on at home. You don't see the battles they're fighting silently. You don't see the insecurities behind their jokes, their silence, or their confidence. Everyone's carrying something they're not showing.

We all want to be understood, not misjudged. So, give others the same grace you'd want if someone only saw a moment of your life and thought that was your whole story.

Judgment closes minds. Curiosity opens hearts.

Instead of judging:
- Pause. Ask: "What don't I know about their story?"
- Remember: You only see a snapshot.
- Give what you want to get—understanding, not criticism.

Optional Reading:
12 Rules for Life by Jordan B. Peterson.

This isn't an easy read, it's deep, sometimes heavy, but it's powerful. It structures a messy world and reminds you that your choices matter. Even if you don't read the whole thing now, just one or two of the rules (like "Stand up straight" or "Tell the truth") might stay with you forever.

Come back to it when you're older or life feels chaotic, and you need a bit of order. It helped me, and I reckon it could help you too.

JOY

Joy isn't something that just shows up when life is perfect—because let's be honest, life rarely is. Joy is something you choose to notice, even in the middle of the mess. It often lives in the small stuff: your favourite song at the right moment, a deep laugh with a friend, sunlight through your window, or the feeling of being completely yourself, even just for a second.

You don't have to wait for a big achievement or a "perfect day" to feel joy. In fact, the people who are happiest often aren't the ones with the easiest lives, they're the ones who've learned how to find joy in ordinary moments.

Protect your joy. Don't let the world make you feel bad for smiling too wide, laughing too loud, or celebrating something small. Joy isn't selfish, it's fuel. And in a world that can sometimes feel heavy, joy is an act of strength.

Make space for it. Notice it. *Choose* it.

Quote to Remember
"Judgment divides. Jealousy distracts. But joy? Joy heals everything." — Liam Mulhall

Task: Jealousy Flip & Joy Hunt

1. Flip the Feeling
Think of someone you feel jealous of. Maybe it's a classmate who always seems confident, a friend who's getting more attention, or someone online who looks like they have it all.

Now write their name down, just for you. Instead of sitting in jealousy, *flip it*. Ask yourself:

What do I admire about them?

What are three qualities or things they have that I wish I had too?

What's one small way I can start growing those same things in *my* life, in my own way?

This isn't about copying them. It's about turning jealousy into a signal, then using that signal to guide your growth.

2. Go on a Joy Hunt
Set a timer for fifteen minutes. Your goal? Find or create three small moments of joy.

It could be:
- Dancing in your room with music up loud.
- Sending a meme to a mate.
- Walking outside and feeling the sun on your face.
- Watching something that makes you laugh.
- Writing, painting, or kicking a footy around.

Joy doesn't need to be huge or loud, it just needs to be *felt*. And the more you practice finding it, the easier it gets.

K KINDNESS, KARMA, KNOWLEDGE

Story: The Ripple Effect

Haylee didn't think much of it when she helped a year seven kid pick up his books after someone knocked them over. It was just a small act. No big deal.

But a week later, that same kid helped someone else, thinking of Haylee who had helped him without asking for anything in return. Then *that* person passed the kindness on, inspired by the kid's quiet example.

Haylee didn't know it at the time, but she'd started a ripple. One small moment of kindness created a chain reaction, not because it was loud or flashy, but because it was real.

Advice & Wisdom

KINDNESS

Kindness isn't a weakness, it's strength in action. It means helping someone without needing recognition. It's doing the right thing when no one's clapping. Real kindness isn't about what you get back, it's about who you choose to be.

That's the heart of karma, the idea that the energy you put into the world often finds its way back to you. Not through magic, but through how people respond, how doors open, and how your choices shape the world around you.

What does kindness look like?
- Saying thank you and meaning it.
- Holding the door open for someone else.
- Smiling at someone who looks down on you.
- Messaging a mate to check in.
- Letting someone else speak without interrupting.
- Giving someone the benefit of the doubt.
- Choosing not to post something cruel, even if it's funny.

Kindness doesn't cost much. But it's always worth it, what goes around comes around!

KARMA

You never know where your ripple will land. Today's small act of kindness might change someone's whole day—maybe even their whole life.

If you've ever seen the *Thai Life Insurance* ad, the one where a man quietly helps others every day, you'll know exactly what I mean. He waters a plant, feeds a stray dog, helps an elderly vendor. No applause. No rewards. Just kindness, repeated.

If you haven't seen it yet, look it up. It'll teach you more about the power of kindness in three minutes than most people learn in thirty years.

Quote to Remember
"Be kind even when no one's watching. Be hungry to learn. And remember—every action plants a seed." — Liam Mulhall

Task: Knowledge List & Kindness Chain

1. Knowledge List
Write down three things you want to understand better. It could be anything that matters to you, like:

- How to deal with anxiety.
- How to build healthy relationships.
- How to save and manage money.
- How to start a business or side hustle.
- How to build confidence.
- How your brain or body works.
- How to cook something simple.

Now, pick one. Spend just twenty minutes today learning about it.

How?
- Watch a YouTube video from someone you trust.
- Listen to a podcast on the topic.
- Read an article or book chapter.
- Ask someone older who knows more.
- Use a learning app.

You don't need all the answers today, but every bit of knowledge adds power to your toolkit. The more you know, the stronger you grow.

2. Kindness Chain
Do one kind thing today and don't tell anyone.

Help with a chore without being asked. Send a message to someone who's been quiet lately. Let someone go ahead of you. Pay someone a genuine compliment. Leave a kind note on someone's desk or locker. Smile at a stranger who looks like they need it.

The rule? No recognition. No posting. No looking for a thank you.

And here's the twist, when you do that one kind thing, ask the person—if it makes sense—to pass it on. Tell them: "Someone helped me today, and I just wanted to pay it forward. If you can, do something kind for someone else."

That's how kindness spreads, like a chain. Quiet. Powerful. Unstoppable

KNOWLEDGE

Knowledge gives you options and that creates freedom. The more you learn, the more choices you have. Choices about how you think, how you respond, and where your life can go.

Some people hear the word "knowledge" and think of grades, textbooks, or who can memorise the most facts for a test. But that's just one part of it.

What really matters is what you learn from living, from conversations, mistakes, questions, and moments that challenge you. It's the kind of learning you do when no one's watching and there's no exam to pass, just a better version of you to grow into.

It's what you pick up when:
- You fail and figure out why.
- You ask questions even when you're scared to sound dumb.
- You realise someone's mistreating you, and decide you deserve better.
- You look up something random just because you're curious.

That's knowledge, too! You don't have to be a straight-A student to be smart. Einstein said, "If you judge a fish by its ability to climb a tree, it will live its whole life believing it's stupid." Maybe school hasn't shown you your strengths yet. Perhaps you think you're not smart because you can't sit still in class or struggle with tests. But there are different types of intelligence—creative, emotional, musical, mechanical, spiritual, athletic, and logical.

Some of the most intelligent people in the world failed school but crushed it in life because they kept learning, just in their way.

The cool thing about knowledge? No one can take it from you. Money can be stolen. Looks fade. Popularity can disappear overnight. But knowledge? Once you've learned something, *really* learned it, it's yours to keep. No one can take it from you. And the more you learn, the more confident you become. You don't have to bluff your way through life or pretend you know things. You'll truly know them.

So, stay curious. Read the book. Ask the awkward question. Look at both sides of a story. Talk to people older, younger, and different from you. Learn from failure, mistakes, and moments you wish you could take back.

Knowledge isn't just about grades or intelligence, it's what helps you make better choices, understand the world around you, and live life on *your* terms. That's real freedom.

L LOVE, LOYALTY, LONELINESS

Story: The Empty Room

Manny was surrounded by teammates, classmates, and online "friends." But one night, after a big game, he sat alone in his room and felt... hollow.

It wasn't the attention he lacked. It was a *connection*. That night, he messaged his sister. Just two words: "You up?"

They talked. About real stuff. About feelings. It didn't fix everything. But it reminded him he wasn't alone.

Advice & Wisdom

LOVE

Real love *respects* you. It doesn't try to control you. It doesn't make you feel guilty for having your own life, your own space, or your own friends. It doesn't demand constant attention or proof that you care.

Love is different from obsession or passion. Passion can be intense and exciting, but it can also fade fast or switch to someone else. Real love isn't just about butterflies or drama. It's about trust, effort, and supporting each other, even on the boring or hard days.

Love also isn't the same as attachment. Attachment comes from fear, like being scared to be alone or worrying someone will leave. That kind of love holds on too tight. Real love gives you room to breathe, to grow, and to be fully *you.*

If someone truly loves you, they want the best for you, not just what's best for *them*. And that kind of love is worth waiting for.

Things to know about love:
- You don't have to earn it—the real kind shows up, stays, and grows.
- Love includes self-love—how you treat yourself sets the standard.
- You are worthy of a love that feels safe, not scary.

LOYALTY

Loyalty is one of those words we throw around a lot but rarely explore it deeper. It's easy to say "I'm loyal" but it's much harder to accept that loyalty doesn't always look the same from both sides. You might stay up all night supporting someone through their breakup, while they think loyalty means defending them in a group chat. You might forgive someone a hundred times because you love them, and they might think silence is loyalty, never saying the hard truths.

Here's the thing: everyone brings their definition of loyalty into relationships, shaped by their past, their wounds, and what they've seen growing up. Don't assume that just because you're loyal in your way, someone else will be the same in theirs. And don't confuse loyalty with self-abandonment. Staying faithful to someone who repeatedly disrespects your boundaries isn't strength, it's self-betrayal.

Be loyal, yes. But also, be clear. Know what you mean by loyalty. Communicate it. And remember: the most important loyalty is the one you hold with yourself.

LONELINESS

You can be surrounded by a crowd and still feel completely alone. That's because loneliness isn't always about who's near you, it's about who *truly understands* you. At its core, loneliness is a disconnection. Not from the world, but from feeling seen, heard, and valued in it.

We all feel lonely sometimes—that's human. But try not to *live* in that space. There's a difference between solitude and loneliness: one is a choice, the other is a longing. Solitude can be peaceful. Loneliness can feel hollow.

Don't just fill your life with people. Nurture real connections. Be conscious about who you open up to and how you stay connected. That's what protects you from loneliness, even in the busiest rooms.

Tips to combat it:
- Connect deeply, not widely.
- Speak up about how you feel—someone else likely feels the same.
- Find your "soul-fuel" people, the ones who light you up.

Quote to Remember
"Love is not pain. Loyalty is not blind. Loneliness is not forever—but honesty will always bring you closer to connection." — Liam Mulhall

Task: Love Check-In & Connection Reach-Out

1. Self-Love Check-In:
Write down three ways you can be kinder to yourself this week. Then pick one and do it.

2. Reach Out:
Send a message to someone you care about: "I just wanted to say I appreciate you." You never know who needs to hear it.

M MENTAL HEALTH, MATERIALISM, MINDFULNESS, MONEY

Story: The Mask of "I'm Fine"

One night, she turned off her phone. Just turned it off. No posts, no scrolling, no pretending. She sat on her floor in silence and cried.

The tears came quietly at first, then all at once. Her chest ached, her throat tightened, but she didn't stop them. It felt like something heavy was finally lifting. For the first time in months, she wasn't performing. She wasn't pushing through. She was just *being*. And with every tear, her breath came easier. Slower. Real.

Advice & Wisdom

MENTAL HEALTH

Taking care of your mind is just as important as looking after your body. You don't have to be in crisis to check in with your mental health. In fact, the best time to care for it is *before* things get too overwhelming.

Good mental health doesn't mean you're always happy. It means you have space to feel your emotions, tools to cope with stress, and people you can talk to when life feels heavy. It's about balance, getting enough rest, setting boundaries, staying connected, and giving yourself permission to slow down when you need to.

Just like you'd see a doctor if you had a broken arm, it's okay and important to ask for help when your thoughts or feelings feel out of control. There's no shame in that. It's strength. Your mental health is part of your health.

Protect it by:
- Getting enough sleep.
- Talking instead of bottling.
- Moving your body.
- Saying "no" when something drains you.

If you wish to better understand your mind and improve your mental health, the patterns you've developed from childhood, the emotional habits you repeat, and how to break those cycles, Dr. Nicole LePera's *How to Do the Work* is one of the best books I've ever read to help me understand myself.

Feeling better is important, but it's only part of the process. Real healing begins when you understand where your pain is coming from. When you stop just covering it up and start working through it. That's how you learn, grow, and begin to feel whole again.

And if what you're feeling doesn't go away after a day or two, if it's more than just a rough patch, please don't try to handle it all by yourself. If you're feeling constantly tired, easily overwhelmed, disconnected from the people around you, or like nothing really matters anymore, those are signs your mind and body are asking for help. And that's okay.

If you're struggling to eat, sleep, focus, or enjoy things you used to care about, you deserve support, not shame. Asking for help isn't weakness. It's one of the strongest and bravest things you can do.

Talk to someone you trust, like a parent, a school counsellor, a teacher, a coach, or a doctor. You don't have to know exactly what to say, just start with, "I haven't been feeling like myself lately." That's enough.

There is also professional support like psychologists, helplines, and youth mental health services. They're there because what you're feeling is real, and you don't have to carry it alone.

Need Support?
- Kids Helpline (Australia): 1800 55 1800, 24/7, free, private.
- Lifeline: 13 11 14.

MATERIALISM

Let's be honest—being a teenager today is like standing in a never-ending ad. Social media, pop culture, even your schoolyard, everywhere you look, someone's flashing the "must-haves." The right clothes, the newest phone, the best car. It's easy to feel like your value comes from what you wear, what you drive, or how much money you've got.

But that's the trap. What's popular today will be old news tomorrow. Your self-worth isn't tied to a logo on your shirt or the number of followers. Actual value, the kind that lasts, comes from how you treat people, especially those with less than you.

Materialism often hides insecurity. We chase "stuff" hoping it will make us feel powerful, accepted, or admired. But that feeling fades—it always does. That psychological process, where the excitement or happiness fades after getting something new, is called *hedonistic adaptation*. The high wears off. The thing that once made you feel amazing quickly becomes your new normal.

Here's a truth: some of the happiest people in the world have very little, but they're content, and some of the wealthiest people are miserable because they're always chasing the next thing. Be someone who values hard work, gratitude, and what you already have. Respect what your family can give you, even if it's not everything. Behind many young people who achieve something big, whether it's in school, sport, art, or life, there's often a parent, carer, or guardian who gave up a lot to make it possible—time, money, sleep, comfort, dreams of their own. Their sacrifices may not always be seen, but they shape everything.

Stuff doesn't make you valuable. Character does.

MINDFULNESS

Life moves fast. Your mind races ahead, your heart gets stuck in the past, and before you know it, you've missed the moment you're in. That's where mindfulness comes in.

What is mindfulness? It's not about some meditation pose or lighting candles—though that's fine, too. Mindfulness is simply paying purposeful attention to what's happening without judging it.

Imagine turning the light on in a dark room. Suddenly, you can see clearly. That's what mindfulness does, it lets you notice things just as they are, instead of reacting to what you *think* they are.

Try this, use your senses to ground yourself:
- What can you see?
- What can you hear?
- What can you feel?
- What can you smell?
- What can you taste?

This pulls your brain out of the panic or overthinking loop and back into the present.

Why does this matter? Mindfulness helps you manage anxiety, calm anger, and feel more in control. It's like a mental muscle—the more you practice, the stronger it gets.

Quote to Remember
"You are not your mind's mess. You are not your stuff. You are awareness itself—awake, alive, and enough." — Liam Mulhall

Task: Digital Detox & Mindful Moment

1. Phone-Free Hour:
Choose one hour today. No phone, no screen. Do something physical, creative, or calm, and try one hour before bed to have no screens. The blue light from screens disrupts melatonin production, your body's natural sleeping tablet, making it harder to fall asleep.

2. 5-4-3-2-1 Grounding Exercise:
Name:
- Five things you see.
- Four things you can touch.
- Three things you hear.
- Two things you smell.
- One thing you're grateful for.

MONEY

It's not everything, but it affects everything. Money might not buy happiness, but it does buy freedom, safety, options, and opportunities. And let's be honest, that matters.

Some people grow up with a lot of money and never think twice about spending it. Others grow up with very little and learn to be cautious, frugal, or anxious about every cent. Your relationship with money is shaped early, but it can be re-shaped anytime, especially if you're open to learning how it works.

Here's the truth; if you learn to manage money while still young, you'll save yourself a lot of stress later in life. And no, this doesn't mean you must become obsessed with getting rich. It just means understanding money as a tool that can either work for you or trap you if you don't respect it.

Here are three books I recommend if you're open to learning more:

Rich Dad, Poor Dad by Robert Kiyosaki. A classic that flips the way you see work, school, and money.

The Barefoot Investor by Scott Pape. A practical, Aussie-friendly guide that teaches you how to handle your money from your first job into adulthood.

The Psychology of Money by Morgan Housel. This one dives deep into why people make the money decisions they do. It's more about mindset than maths and is one of the most eye-opening books I've read.

If you pick up even just one idea from these books, it could change how you view your future. Financial independence means having control over your choices, how you spend, where you live, and what you do. It's not always about having *more* money. It's about learning how to manage what you have so you're not stuck relying on others or feeling trapped.

Quick Task: Start Your Money Map

Take ten minutes and try this simple exercise:
- Write down three things you've spent money on last week. It could be food, games, clothes, subscriptions, anything.
- Ask yourself: Were they wants or needs? There's no right or wrong answer, just be honest.

- Now write down one thing you'd like to save for. A concert, a trip, a car, even your future self, whatever feels important.
- Estimate how much it costs and how long it might take you to save. This is your first mini money goal.

Reflection Questions

What kind of relationship do I want with money—stressful, free, generous, intelligent? Why?

What's one lesson about money I wish someone had taught me earlier, or I want to remember now?

N NEGATIVITY, NUDITY (ONLINE), NEEDS VS. WANTS

Story: The Photo He Couldn't Take Back

Ty sent a nude picture because he thought it would make his crush like him more. She sent one back. It felt exciting—until it didn't. A week later, someone else had it, and then more people. The messages turned cruel. His heart sank every time his phone buzzed.

It was just a moment, but it changed everything.

Advice & Wisdom

NEGATIVITY

Let go of bitterness. Holding on to bitterness, resentment, or grudges might feel like power, like you're standing your ground or refusing to let someone off the hook. But really, it's like drinking poison and hoping the other person gets sick.

That kind of pain doesn't hurt them, it hurts *you*. It weighs you down. It follows you into your thoughts, your relationships, your day-to-day mood. And over time, it starts to shape how you see the world. You become guarded, angry, and tired.

Letting go doesn't mean what they did was okay. It means you're not letting it control you anymore. Forgiveness, when you're ready, isn't for them, it's for *you*. It's freedom.

Negativity doesn't make you strong. Being negative all the time doesn't mean you're realistic or tough, it just makes everything feel heavier. Constant criticism, sarcasm, or expecting the worst doesn't protect you from pain. It just makes it harder to enjoy the good stuff when it comes.

Real strength is being open enough to hope. To care. To try. Staying kind in a hard world is powerful. Staying soft when life wants to make you hard, *that's* real toughness.

To flip the script:
- Catch your inner critic.

That voice in your head that tells you you're not good enough, smart enough, attractive enough, that's your inner critic. Everyone has one. The trick is learning how to spot it, so it doesn't run the show.

Give it a name if it helps, something silly like "Doubtzilla" or "Negative Nancy." That small act of naming makes it easier to separate those thoughts from who *you* really are. You are not your inner critic.

Next, challenge it. If your inner voice says, "I always mess things up," reframe it into "I made a mistake, but I can learn from it." If it says, "Nobody likes me," reframe it into "I'm still figuring out who my people are, and that's okay."

The goal isn't to fake confidence. It's to be fair to yourself.

- Choose honest people, not just cheerleaders.

You deserve people who support you but not people who lie to protect your feelings. Real friends lift you *by telling the truth kindly*. They celebrate your wins, call you out when you're off track, and stay in your corner when things get hard.

Avoid people who constantly put others down, mock effort, or act like they're "too cool" to care. But also, beware of the ones who only flatter, agree with everything you say, and never give real feedback. That's not loyalty. That's manipulation.

Look for people who challenge you to be better, not just to feel better.

- Don't tear others down to feel tall.

Being kind doesn't mean you're soft. It means you're strong enough not to need to crush someone else to feel important. Mocking, gossiping, or putting people down might get a quick laugh or make you feel powerful for a second, but it costs you something every time. Respect. Integrity. Trust.

True confidence is quiet. It lets others shine too.

NUDITY ONLINE

You are not a product. Your body is not currency. Your worth isn't measured in pictures, likes, or messages.

Before sending anything intimate, pause and ask yourself:

- Is this something I truly want to do, or is it something I feel pressured into?
- Would I still feel okay if this photo or message were shared without my consent?
- Does this person make me feel safe, respected, and in control?

These questions aren't meant to scare you, they're meant to protect you. Consent still matters, even with a screen between you. Just because it happens online doesn't make it any less real. Consent isn't only about physical contact, it matters just as much in your DMs, your texts, and your snaps.

No one should ever pressure you to send something that makes you uncomfortable, not even someone you care about, not even if they say "Everyone does it." That pressure isn't love, it's manipulation. If someone is asking for nudes or sexual content and you feel nervous, unsure, or pressured, stop.

For Girls and Young Women
Many girls are pressured into sending nudes to prove something, like to show they like someone, to stay in a relationship, or just to avoid being left out or labelled.

But here's the truth: Your body is not proof of love. Your comfort is not something to trade for attention. You don't owe anyone access to your body, online or offline.

For Boys and Young Men
You may feel like sending nudes or sexual messages is bold, expected, or part of flirting. But if someone didn't ask, don't send. It's not brave. It's crossing a line. Respect means *waiting for clear consent*, not assuming it.

Being a man isn't about taking what you want. It's about knowing when not to.

If You're Unsure, Wait
You are allowed to say no. You are allowed to change your mind, even after saying yes. You are allowed to block someone, report someone, or stop talking to someone who makes you feel unsafe.

Holding yourself back takes more strength than giving in. And if someone pushes you past your "no," that's not a healthy relationship. That's a red flag. If it wouldn't feel okay in person, it's not okay online either.

Consent is clear, mutual, and never pressured.

NEEDS VS. WANTS

Needs vs. Wants: What Really Fuels You
Some things we need to survive and thrive. Other things we want because they feel good in the moment. Both are okay. But knowing the difference helps you stay grounded when life gets loud and distracting.

Needs Are Your Foundation
Needs keep you steady physically, emotionally, and mentally. They don't always feel exciting, but they give your life strength and stability.

Examples of real needs:
- Connection—feeling understood, supported, and accepted.
- Purpose—doing something meaningful, even if it's small.
- Rest—sleep, stillness, and space to recharge.
- Food—not just eating but fuelling your body with what it truly needs.
- Movement—walking, stretching, dancing, training.
- Love—kindness, belonging, and knowing you're enough.

When your needs are met, you don't just survive, you feel stronger, more focused, and more *you*.

Wants Are Louder But They Don't Last
Wants can be fun. They often give you a quick boost, but the feeling fades fast. There's nothing wrong with wanting things. The problem is when you start chasing *wants* instead of meeting your *needs*.

Common wants:
- More likes or followers.
- New clothes or the latest phone.
- Fast compliments or validation.
- Fitting in with trends, even if it's not really you.
- Constant entertainment or distraction.

None of these are "bad." But if you ignore your needs while chasing wants, life starts to feel hollow like you're always reaching for something but never quite full.

Needs vs. Wants In Real Life
Here's what it looks like in action:
- You need real friends who support you. You might *want* followers who hype you up but they won't be there when you're hurting. Real friends will.
- You need rest. You might *want* to scroll social media until two in the morning but sleep will make tomorrow better. The feed won't.
- You need to be proud of who you are. You might *want* someone's approval but their opinion fades. Self-respect sticks.

How to Check in With Yourself
Ask:
- Am I chasing something that looks good or something that feels right?
- Will this leave me feeling more whole, or more drained?
- Have I met my needs today or am I running on empty?
- Even just *asking* those questions can shift your focus and give you clarity. Wants are fun. Needs are fuel. Don't trade one for the other.

Quote to Remember
"You're allowed to want. But don't forget what you truly need—safety, peace, and self-worth." — Liam Mulhall

Task: Wants vs. Needs List
Draw two columns:
- Wants—things you desire, enjoy, or crave.
- Needs—what your body, mind, and heart genuinely require.

Now circle three needs. Choose *one small thing* you can do today to honour each one.

O OVERTHINKING, OPENNESS, ONLINE LIFE

Story: The Spiral That Stole Sleep

Noah couldn't sleep. His brain wouldn't shut up—replaying every awkward moment from the day, imagining every possible disaster tomorrow. He was stuck in a loop. It felt like control… but it was chaos.

The spiral slowed when he finally started journaling—dumping his thoughts without judgment. It wasn't gone. But it no longer owned him.

Advice & Wisdom

OVERTHINKING

Your brain's job is to think. That includes helpful thoughts… and not-so-helpful ones.

Some thoughts guide you. Others distract you. And some can be downright mean. But just because a thought shows up in your head doesn't mean it's true.

You might think:
- "I'm not good enough."
- "Everyone's judging me."
- "I always mess things up."
- "Nothing's ever going to get better."

These thoughts can *feel* real but that doesn't mean they *are* real. Think of your thoughts like pop-up windows. Some are useful. Others are just noise. The power comes from learning to notice your thoughts without letting them control you.

When Overthinking Takes Over

Instead of instantly believing every thought, try this:
- Pause. Ask: Is this thought helping or hurting me right now?
- Challenge it. What would I say to a friend who thought this about themselves?
- Redirect it. Replace it with something honest and fair, not fake positivity, just balance.

For example:
- "I'm such a failure." → "I've made mistakes, but I can try again."
- "Nobody likes me." → "I'm still finding my people and that takes time."

Remember:
- Your thoughts are *part* of you but they don't define you.
- You are the thinker, not the thought.

Break the Loop

When overthinking spirals, do something to interrupt the cycle:
- Write it down. Get the clutter out of your head and onto paper.
- Ask yourself: Is this true? Is this helpful? Can I act on it?
- Move your body. Go for a walk, stretch, dance. Overthinking hates motion.
- Replace "what if" with "even if."

"What if I fail?" becomes "Even if I fail, I'll learn something." "What if they laugh at me?" becomes "Even if they do, I'll still be proud I tried."

"What if" thinking feeds anxiety. It tries to control the future. "Even if" thinking builds resilience. It reminds you that whatever happens, you can handle it.

OPENNESS

It's okay not to have all the answers. Seriously, no one does. And pretending you do only closes the door to learning.

Being open doesn't mean you're weak or unsure. It means you're *teachable*. It means you're willing to listen, to grow, and to admit when you don't know something. That takes *real* strength. You don't have to be the loudest voice in the room to be respected. In fact, people often respect those who stay curious, ask thoughtful questions, and admit when they're wrong.

Openness isn't about always agreeing, it's about being *willing* to consider a new perspective. It's not changing who you are. It's expanding who you're becoming. In a world where everyone wants to be right, be someone who wants to learn. That mindset will take you further than pride ever could.

ONLINE LIFE

It's real and it's not. What you post online is a part of you. The laughs, the photos, the opinions, they're real. But social media only shows *moments*, not the full story.

It's easy to forget that what we see is carefully chosen, edited, filtered, and sometimes performed. Comparing your behind-the-scenes to someone else's highlight reel will always leave you feeling like you're not enough.

Likes aren't love. Shares aren't self-worth. A post going viral might feel good. A post getting ignored might sting. But neither defines your value. The number of hearts on a photo doesn't reflect the size of your heart. You are more than your followers, more than your feed, and more than the version of you that fits inside a caption.

Online life is real but it's not *everything*. Let it be part of your world, not the centre of it.

Tips for Online Sanity
- Curate your feed like you curate your friends.

The content you scroll through everyday shapes how you think, feel, and see yourself. If someone consistently makes you feel small, anxious, or not good enough, you should unfollow them, even if they're popular.

Follow accounts that lift you up, educate you, or reflect the kind of energy you want more of. Your online space should feel safe, not suffocating.

- Take breaks. Constant input dulls your soul.

Being plugged in 24/7 doesn't leave space to *feel*. It's okay to be bored. In fact, boredom is powerful. It gives your mind space to breathe, to imagine, and to reset.

Some of your most creative ideas and emotional breakthroughs will come when the screen is off.

Don't measure your life in likes.

Your worth isn't tied to how many views, followers, or shares you get. It's not really about the pixels, it's the *pressure*. The pressure to be seen. To be perfect. To be enough.

But real life? It's what happens off-screen. The laughter, the quiet talks, the memories no one posts about. Validation from others is temporary. Self-worth? That stays with you.

Quote to Remember
"Not every thought is the truth. Not every opinion needs your energy. And no post defines your worth." — Liam Mulhall

Task: Mind Dump & Social Reset

Mind Dump
Write freely for five to ten minutes. No structure, no filter. Just let your mind exhale.

Social Cleanse
Unfollow five accounts that make you question your worth or drain your energy. Replace them with five that leave you feeling motivated, understood, or at peace.

P PURPOSE, PORN, PEER PRESSURE

Story: Charlotte's Cool Girl Crossroads

Charlotte felt it before she fully understood it.
The way everyone at the table laughed just a bit too loud when the quiet girl dropped her tray.
How no one helped.
How no one *dared* to.

That was the rule, wasn't it? Stay silent. Stay cool. Stay part of the group.

But something in Charlotte shifted.
It wasn't anger that rose in her, but a quiet, solid knowing — the kind that doesn't need permission.

She stood up, walked away from the table, and sat down beside the girl they'd targeted.

It was awkward at first.
Then the girl gave her a small smile. "Thanks," she whispered.

And just like that, Charlotte didn't feel like she was on the outside.
She felt like she was finally where she belonged.

They started eating lunch together. Shared inside jokes. Spoke honestly.
No filters. No fake laughs. No pressure.

Over time, they became inseparable, not because they wore the right clothes or had the right friends,
but because they truly understood each other.

And as the years passed, Charlotte learned something powerful:
The girl who once sat alone had one of the kindest hearts and sharpest minds she'd ever known.

They helped each other through everything — exams, heartbreak, self-doubt, and growing up.

Charlotte never regretted leaving that lunch table.
Because the day she chose kindness over popularity,
she didn't just make a friend, she found her people.

And that made all the difference.

Advice & Wisdom

PURPOSE

Your purpose isn't a job title. It's what makes you feel *alive*. It's that spark you feel when you're helping, building, imagining, or expressing something that matters to you.

You don't have to know your entire life plan right now. Most people don't. But you can start by asking the right questions.

What do you love to create, solve, help, or express? That's not just a hobby, that's a clue. Follow it. To start discovering your purpose, try asking yourself:

- What breaks your heart, and what would you fix if you could?

Pain is often a compass. If something deeply bothers you, like unfairness, loneliness, waste, or silence, maybe you're meant to be part of the solution.

- What would you do even if no one clapped?

If applause disappeared, what would you keep doing? That's where passion lives, in the quiet, when no one's watching.

What do people always come to you for?

Advice? Creativity? Support? Problem-solving? Your natural gifts often show up in what others notice, even if you don't see it yet.

Purpose doesn't arrive fully formed. It's not a lightning bolt, it's a slow build. It's shaped by curiosity, courage, and small steps taken again and again.   Try things. Mess up. Learn. Say yes to what lights you up. Say no to what dims you.

And remember: your purpose doesn't have to be loud to matter, it just must be *true to you*.

PORN

It's everywhere, on your phone, in memes, ads, social media, even jokes. And while it might seem normal or even harmless, *porn isn't without consequences*. This isn't about shame. It's about *awareness*.

Here's what porn doesn't teach you:
- Real intimacy—the kind built on trust, vulnerability, and emotional connection.
- Respect—for your body, their body, and the space between.
- Consent—understanding, asking, and honouring boundaries.
- Communication—being able to talk honestly about what you want, need, and feel.

Porn doesn't show you the awkwardness, care, laughter, or trust that makes real intimacy meaningful.

It can quietly shape how you view sex, relationships, and even yourself without you noticing. Over time, it can mess with your brain's reward system, rewiring how you experience desire, connection, and satisfaction. Real-life connection can start to feel dull in comparison to constant, artificial stimulation.

You might find yourself chasing the next high but feeling emptier after.

Ask yourself:
- Is this shaping how I treat people or what I expect from them?
- Is it replacing real connection in my life?
- Do I feel more whole after watching, or more disconnected?

There's nothing wrong with curiosity. But there *is* strength in self-reflection. You don't need to feel ashamed. But it's worth asking: "Is this helping me grow, or keeping me stuck?"

You're not defined by your habits. You're defined by your willingness to *question* them. There's real courage in stepping back and choosing something better than a screen, something real, kind, and deeply human.

PEER PRESSURE

You don't need to shrink yourself to fit in. Sometimes saying "no" makes you stronger than any "yes."

Peer pressure isn't always loud it can be quiet glances, off-hand comments, or the fear of being left out. It's the subtle feeling that if you just go along with everyone else, you'll belong. But here's the truth: if you must change who you are to be accepted, it's not real acceptance.

When pressure hits:
- Pause. Breathe. Ask: "Is this true to me? Does this feel like my *authentic* self?" In that moment, you get to choose who's really in control—the crowd, or your conscience.

- Remember: The people who genuinely care about you won't pressure you to be smaller, quieter, or less than who you are. Real friends don't just want you around, they want the *real you* around.
- Your gut knows—trust it. That twist in your stomach? That hesitation? That's your inner voice asking for a moment of courage. Don't ignore it.

It takes strength to stand your ground in a world that rewards going with the flow. But every time you honour your truth, you build confidence.

You don't have to be aggressive just clear. "No thanks." "I'm not into that." "I'm good." That's all it takes. And the more you say it, the easier it gets.

Quote to Remember
"Your purpose is personal. Your choices are powerful. Your worth isn't up for vote." — Liam Mulhall

Task: Purpose Map & Pressure Check

1. Purpose Map:

Write these down:
- Things I enjoy.
- Things I'm good at.
- Things the world needs.

Look for the overlap. That's your compass.

2. Pressure Check:

List three times you gave in to pressure. Now rewrite what you *wish* you'd said. Practice using that voice the next time.

 QUESTIONS, QUEERNESS, QUIET TIME

Story: The Question That Freed Her

Lani wrote the question in her journal for the first time: "What if I'm not straight?"

It scared her—not because she had an answer, but because she didn't. Still, the more she returned to the question, the more honest she became with herself.

It wasn't about putting a label on it. It was about finally telling the truth. And that truth felt like a deep exhale after holding her breath for far too long.

Bottom of Form

Advice & Wisdom

QUESTIONS

Good questions change everything. They open doors. They challenge the scripts we've been handed and help us write our own. Asking the right question doesn't mean you're lost, it means you're *thinking*, growing, becoming.

Never be afraid to ask:

- "Why does this matter to me?" Is this goal, opinion, or pressure truly mine—or am I chasing something because I think I'm *supposed* to?
- "Is this belief mine, or was it given to me?" Sometimes we carry beliefs from family, culture, or school that don't fit who we're becoming. You're allowed to question them. You're allowed to change.
- "What do I truly need right now?" Not what others expect. Not what looks good online, but what *you* actually need—which could be rest, connection, space, a fresh start.

You grow through curiosity, not certainty. It's okay not to have all the answers. What matters is that you're *asking better questions*. The people who grow the most aren't the ones who know everything, they're the ones brave enough to explore what they *don't*.

So, keep asking. Keep wondering. That's where the real learning begins.

QUEERNESS

Who you love, how you identify, that's your story. And it's valid.

You don't need to fit a label right away. You don't need to have all the answers. You're allowed to explore who you are emotionally, romantically, and physically and take your time doing it.

If you're exploring your identity:
- There's no deadline. Your identity can evolve, shift, or stay exactly the same. It's yours.
- You don't owe anyone an explanation, especially if you're still figuring it out.
- You deserve spaces where you feel safe, respected, and seen for *all* of who you are.

- You can explore what feels right to you as long as everything is legal, safe, and based on *clear, mutual consent.*

If someone shares their identity with you:
- Thank them. Sharing something personal means they trust you. Don't take that lightly.
- Use the name and pronouns they give you. Even if it takes time to adjust, make the effort.
- Don't ask invasive questions. Let them share what they're comfortable sharing.
- Be the safe space they hope you'll be; open, respectful, and kind.

You don't have to fully understand someone to treat them with compassion. The goal isn't perfection, it's respect. And the most powerful way to support someone is to let them be *exactly who they are*, without fear.

QUIET TIME

Silence isn't emptiness. Solitude isn't loneliness. Stillness gives you the space to hear your thoughts — without the noise of the world constantly telling you who to be.

We spend so much of life plugged in: scrolling, reacting, filling every quiet moment with distraction. But growth often happens in the gaps, in the pauses we usually try to avoid.

Why slowing down matters:
- It reduces stress by calming your nervous system.
- It gives you room to reflect, reset, and make clearer decisions.
- It boosts creativity—some of your best insights come when the world goes quiet.

What might get in the way:
- At first, silence can feel awkward, even uncomfortable.
- Your mind may race with things you've been too busy to face.
- The urge to check your phone might be automatic.

That's okay. The goal isn't to clear your mind or feel Zen, it's simply to *notice*. Start small: two minutes. Then five. Then ten. Think of stillness like a muscle. It strengthens with use.

Try this:
- Put your phone away for ten minutes.
- Journal what's on your mind—messy, honest, whatever comes.
- Sit outside. Breathe. Let yourself *notice* the sounds, the colours, the sky.

Quiet time isn't isolation, it's coming home to yourself. It's not about doing it, it's about being present. And the more comfortable you get with that stillness, the more clearly your inner voice will speak.

Quote to Remember
"Your questions are holy. Your identity is sacred. And your quiet moments hold the loudest truths." — Liam Mulhall

Task: Journal Your Question
Write down five questions you've been afraid to ask—the big ones, the private ones. Let them sit. Don't rush the answers. Let them guide you.

Then, spend ten minutes alone. No music. No phone. Just you, your breath, and the stillness. You might be surprised at what rises to the surface.

R RESILIENCE, RESPECT, REST, RELATIONSHIPS

Story: The Bounce-Back Moment

Theo failed a significant test. His parents were disappointed, and he felt like a total loser. But instead of hiding, he met with his teacher, acknowledged his failure, and made a new plan.

He passed the resit two months later. But the real win wasn't the grade — it was the comeback. That's what resilience looks like.

Advice & Wisdom

RESILIENCE

You will fall. You will get hurt. You will lose. But resilience means you *get back up*, even if it takes time.

- Fail forward.

Failure isn't the end, it's feedback. Failing forward means learning something from every setback and using it to grow. It's saying, "Okay, that didn't work, but here's what I'll do differently next time." Every mistake moves you one step closer to understanding, confidence, and success.

- Learn from the pain.

Pain teaches you things comfort can't. Whether it's heartbreak, disappointment, or rejection, those experiences shape your strength. They show you where your boundaries are, what matters most to you, and how you bounce back. You don't have to love the pain, but you *can* learn from it.

- Ask for help when you need it.

You don't have to carry everything on your own. Asking for support isn't weakness, it's wisdom. Whether it's a friend, teacher, parent, or counsellor, reaching out is a sign of courage and self-respect. Everyone needs help sometimes, even the strongest people lean on others.

- Trust that you can handle hard things.

You've already survived things you once thought you couldn't. That's proof. Resilience is built when you stay in the fight, even when it's hard. You don't have to feel fearless, you just have to keep going. Step by step, breath by breath.

REST

The best supplement on the planet isn't in a bottle. It's sleep.

If you want more energy, better focus, fewer mood swings, clearer skin, faster recovery, a stronger immune system, and even better memory, then there's one thing that helps with all of those: sleep.

And most teens aren't getting enough of it.

You're not unmotivated, you're developing. Your brain, your body, your emotions, your hormones, everything is in overdrive during these years. That's why teens need around eight to ten hours of sleep a night to thrive.

But instead, most teens are running on empty. Late-night scrolling. Early school starts. Stress. Caffeine. Homework. It all adds up.

Sleep isn't just rest. It's *repair*. During sleep, your brain clears out waste, your muscles rebuild, your mood resets, and your memory sharpens. It's when your body heals and your mind processes everything you've learned.

According to psychiatrist Dr. Daniel Amen, one of the world's top brain health experts, sleeping at least eight hours a night can activate seven hundred and two health-promoting genes.

Miss that? Those same genes start to switch off. Your body becomes more inflamed. Your mood dips. Your energy drops. Focus? Forget it.

So, if you're looking for an edge in life, don't just chase supplements—chase better sleep.

What sleep does for you:
- Boosts memory, focus, and learning.
- Balances mood and emotional regulation.
- Strengthens your immune system.
- Increases growth hormone which helps muscles and bones.
- Helps you deal with stress and recover from workouts.
- Makes your skin clearer and more radiant.
- Sharpens decision-making and creativity.

What happens without it:
- More anxiety and low moods.
- Foggy thinking and forgetfulness.
- Cravings for junk food.
- Higher risk of injury and illness.
- Shorter attention span and more emotional outbursts.

How to sleep better:
- Go to bed and wake up around the same time every day, even on weekends.
- Keep your room cool and dark. Your brain loves sleep caves.
- Wind down before bed. Stretch. Breathe. Read. No screens.
- Don't eat heavy food or chug soft drinks late at night. Your body needs to calm, not crank.
- Move your body during the day. Exercise helps you fall asleep faster and sleep deeper.

Remember this: You don't grow when you're scrolling at one in the morning. You grow when you sleep. Sleep is your body's secret weapon. It fuels your brain. Powers your body. And builds the emotional resilience you'll need for everything ahead.

Love your brain. Protect your peace. And give yourself permission to rest.

RELATIONSHIPS

(The Four Pillars That Actually Matter)

You're not meant to carry everything alone.
Even if you're quiet.
Even if you say, "I'm fine" when you're not.

We all need connection — and not just the Wi-Fi kind, but the real kind. People who listen. People who notice. People who care.

Why Relationships Matter

Healthy friendships, strong family bonds, mentors, or even just one safe person — they all act like an emotional safety net. They remind you that you're not alone in this wild, unpredictable world. And when life gets messy, they're the ones who help you hold it together.

Relationships shape how we see ourselves.
The right ones help you grow.
The wrong ones make you shrink.

That's why who you let close — and how they treat you — matters more than you might think.

But Relationships Aren't Always Easy

Some are one-sided. You give and give, and it never feels like enough.
Some are confusing — hot and cold, kind one day, distant the next.
Some fade. Some hurt. Some leave you wondering if it was ever real.

If you're in a relationship — romantic, friendship, or family — that constantly drains you, disrespects your boundaries, or makes you feel small… it's okay to step back.
Protecting your peace isn't selfish. It's necessary.

And What If You Don't Have Anyone Right Now?

That can feel heavy — like everyone else has their people, but you don't.
But this season won't last forever.

Start with you. Be kind to yourself.
Be someone *you'd* want to hang out with.
Put yourself in places where connection can happen: clubs, sports, interest groups, even safe online spaces. It may take time, but you *will* find your people.

And until then, know this:
Your worth isn't defined by how many friends or followers you have.
You're allowed to be in a season of searching.

The Types of Relationships
- **Friendships** — chosen family, day-to-day support, the ones who get your weird jokes.
- **Family** — not always easy, but often deep and complex.
- **Romantic** — attraction, affection, vulnerability, and mutual respect.
- **Mentors** — people who guide and support your growth.
- **Online** — yes, these can be real, but they still need boundaries and honesty.

No relationship should cost you your peace, your identity, or your self-respect.
The people in your life should challenge you to grow — not pressure you to become someone you're not.

And remember:
Being alone for a while is better than being surrounded by the wrong people.

The Four Pillars of a Real Relationship

Author and coach *Jay Shetty* says real relationships are built on four key pillars — and it makes total sense.

Whether it's friendship, family, or love, the strongest bonds go beyond popularity, attention, or status. They're built on something deeper. Something steady. Here's what those four pillars look like:

1. Care
This is the friend or family member who checks in — not out of politeness, but because they genuinely care.
They're the ones who notice when your energy's off, who sit with you in silence when you're hurting, who send the "just making sure you're okay" texts.

They remind you that you matter — not for what you achieve, but simply because of who you are.

2. Competence
This is the person who helps you grow. They're thinkers, builders, and problem-solvers.
They help you set goals, take action, and level up.
They might give you advice about money, school, mindset, or leadership — or they might just live in a way that makes you want to take your life more seriously.
Being around them makes you feel focused and capable.

3. Character
This is your compass friend. They don't have to be perfect — but they remind you of what truly matters.
They live with honesty, kindness, and integrity.
Being around them makes you want to raise your own standards — not because they pressure you, but because they lead by example.

4. Consistency
They might not always say the perfect thing, but they show up — again and again.
They're the 3 a.m. call when you're falling apart.
They're the steady hand in the chaos.
When others disappear, they stay.
In a world that often forgets to follow through, their loyalty is rare — and powerful.

If someone in your life offers you even *one* of these pillars — appreciate them.
If they offer *two or three* — invest in that bond.
And if you ever meet someone who shows *all four*?

Hold on tight.

Because that's the kind of connection that doesn't just support your life — it helps you become the best version of yourself.

RESPECT

Respect starts with *self*. If you don't respect yourself, you'll tolerate what you shouldn't.

You'll let people talk over you, cross your boundaries, or treat you like an afterthought because part of you believes that's all you deserve.

Self-respect isn't about arrogance. It's about knowing your value even when others don't see it yet. It's saying, "I matter. My time matters. My voice matters." When you carry that belief, the way you let others treat you changes.

Self-respect means:
- Walking away from people who don't treat you with kindness.
- Saying "no" without guilt.
- Holding your own values, even when you're the only one in the room.
- Not needing to be liked by everyone to feel enough.

It's easy to abandon yourself to gain popularity, to laugh at things that make you uncomfortable, say yes when your gut screams no, or stay quiet when you know something's wrong.

But respect isn't about being liked. It's about liking yourself after the moment has passed.

Where do boundaries begin, and where does someone else's freedom end? Your boundaries protect your peace, your energy, and your safety. Someone else's freedom doesn't give them permission to cross those lines.

You can respect someone's right to speak while also choosing to walk away. You can support someone's identity or values without needing to copy them. Respect doesn't mean agreement. It means *coexisting* without control, pressure, or erasure.

Respect means:
- Listening, not just waiting for your turn to speak. Pay attention. Don't assume. Listen to understand, not to argue.
- Honouring consent always. Whether it's physical touch, emotional space, or sharing personal stories, ask first, respect the answer, and never guilt someone into saying yes.
- Speaking without harm, especially when you're giving feedback. You can be honest without being cruel. You can challenge someone without crushing them. Respect means thinking about the *impact* of your words, not just the intention.
- Holding space for difference. People believe different things, look different, love differently, live differently. You don't have to agree with someone's identity to treat them with dignity.

Respect is quiet strength. It's not loud, aggressive, or flashy. It's how you carry yourself. How you speak to the cleaner as well as the CEO. How you hold your ground without needing to put others down. And how you treat yourself when no one's watching.

In a world full of pressure to impress, the most powerful thing you can do is respect yourself enough to stay true, especially when no one's clapping.

Quote to Remember
"Resilience isn't about pretending things don't hurt. It's about being strong enough to feel the pain—and keep going anyway. It's better to be a warrior in a garden than a gardener in a war, because peace requires strength—and strength without peace is just destruction." — Liam Mulhall (adapted from an old proverb)

Task: Resilience Reflection & Relationship Radar

1. Resilience Reflection:

Write about a time you got back up after falling, even if it took a while. What did you learn?

2. Relationship Radar:

Pick one relationship in your life. Ask yourself, "Does this relationship lift me or limit me?" Then ask, "What needs to change, the relationship, or the way I treat it?"

Not every limiting relationship needs to end. Sometimes what's needed is a boundary, a conversation, or space to grow. But if something consistently drains your energy, makes you feel small, or pulls you away from who you want to be, it might be time to re-evaluate how much access that person has to you.

S SELF-ESTEEM, SELF-COMPASSION, SPIRITUALITY, STRESS, SOCIAL MEDIA

Story: The Filtered Life

Aiden scrolled for hours. Everyone seemed to be doing better, looking better, and living larger. He started to feel like his real life wasn't enough, so he posted a picture with heavy filters and a fake caption. It got likes, but it felt… hollow.

Later that night, he deleted it. Not because the likes didn't matter, but because pretending to be someone else mattered even more.

Advice & Wisdom

SELF-ESTEEM

Let's be honest—we can be brutal to ourselves. We beat ourselves up for every mistake. We compare our lives to everyone else's highlight reels. And we carry around this voice that whispers, "You're not enough."

But what if the real glow-up isn't about changing your looks or chasing approval, but about changing how you talk to yourself?

Self-esteem isn't just "confidence." It's how you see yourself. It's knowing your worth, even on your worst day. It's the quiet strength that says, "I matter," even when everything else feels shaky.

But here's the thing: self-esteem needs a teammate. And that teammate is self-compassion.

You won't always get things right. You'll mess up, say the wrong thing, fall short. Self-esteem says, "I'm still valuable." Self-compassion says, "I'm still learning, and that's okay."

That voice in your head? You can't silence it completely, but you *can* train it to be kinder. Not fake positivity. Just fairness. Gentleness. A little grace.

You don't have to wait until you're perfect to like yourself. You don't have to earn your worth, you already have it.

"Talk to yourself like someone you love." —Brené Brown

SELF-COMPASSION

It's meeting yourself where you're at, not with judgment but with kindness. It's saying, "I messed up… but I'm learning. I'm not the mistake—I'm a work in progress."

You wouldn't tell your best mate they're a failure for feeling down or making a mistake, so why say it to yourself?

Real talk: You *will* mess up. You *will* feel like crap sometimes. But that doesn't mean you're broken or unworthy. It means you're alive. You're not a robot, you're a work in progress. And that's a pretty fantastic thing to be.

SHAME

Shame is that heavy, sneaky feeling that says, "There's something wrong with me." It's different from guilt. Guilt says, "I did something wrong." Shame says, "I am something wrong." And that's a lie. But it's one many of us believe, especially when we're young.

Where does shame come from? It can come from being bullied—when people tear you down so often, you start believing them. It can come from making mistakes, especially if no one ever taught you that failing is part of learning. It can come from having secrets, when you feel like you're hiding parts of yourself that others wouldn't accept. Or just from feeling different, like you don't fit the mould, or like you're always on the outside looking in.

But it can also come from *home*. Growing up around constant criticism, never hearing "I'm proud of you," or feeling like love had conditions. It can come from *school*, when you're labelled "the quiet one," "the troublemaker," or "not smart enough," and those labels start to stick. It can come from *religion*, especially when beliefs are used to shame rather than guide, or when you're made to feel like who you are is wrong.

And it can come from *trauma*, things that happened to you that were never your fault, but made you question your worth anyway. It can come from moments when someone made you feel small, embarrassed, or unworthy, and now you carry it quietly, like a brick in your backpack.

You might not even realise it's there. You just know something's weighing you down.

What shame wants: To keep you quiet. To make you isolate. To stop you from reaching out. But what does shame hate? Honesty. Connection. Vulnerability. When you speak the things you're ashamed of to someone who gets it, the weight lifts.

You don't have to put every mistake or hurt on social media. But finding even just *one safe person* to talk to is a game-changer.

You are not your past. Whatever happened *to you* or *because of you* doesn't get to define your future. We all have scars. That doesn't make us damaged—it makes us human. Let go of shame. You're allowed to forgive yourself. You're allowed to move forward.

"Shame is the lie someone told you about yourself." —Anais Nin

SPIRITUALITY

You don't need a church to feel connected, and you don't need religion to be spiritual, though you might find it there.

Spirituality is meaning, purpose, and connection to something greater than yourself. It isn't bound by dogma; it lives in everyday moments.

It might look like prayer or meditation. It might be found in nature, silence, art, or helping others. Service can be a profoundly spiritual act, a way of connecting beyond the self.

Whatever grounds you, whatever draws you closer to that more profound sense of connection, nurture it. Return to it often.

STRESS

Stress gets a bad rap but it's not always bad. In small doses, stress can be a *good* thing. It helps you focus during an exam, gives you adrenaline before a big game, or pushes you to prepare for something important. That's called *acute stress*, short bursts that help you rise to the moment.

But when stress sticks around too long, when there's no off switch, it becomes *chronic stress*, and that's where the trouble begins. Chronic stress steals your joy, wrecks your sleep, messes with your health, and clouds your peace of mind.

You might not be lazy. You might be overwhelmed. There's a significant difference.

Most people today are carrying way more than their nervous systems were designed for—constant notifications, pressure to perform, endless comparisons, and very little rest. It's no wonder you feel like shutting down. That's not weakness, it's your body trying to survive in a system that rarely lets you pause.

When the pressure's high, simplify

When life feels heavy, your brain doesn't need *more*. It needs *clarity*. Here's how to simplify:
- Shrink the task. Break one big overwhelming thing into the smallest next step. Instead of "do assignment," start with "open the doc" or "write one sentence."
- Say no. You don't need to be everywhere or say yes to everything. Protect your energy.
- Cut the noise. Turn off notifications. Close extra tabs. Take a few minutes to unplug—even just five.
- Do one thing at a time. Multitasking isn't always a superpower—it can be a trap. Focus brings calm.

Stress Check

Are you overwhelmed or just under-supported? Here's the difference: If you're doing your best but still feel like you're drowning, you might not need more motivation, you might need *more help*.

Ask yourself:
- Do I have anyone to talk to?
- Can I delegate or ask for support?
- Am I expected to do too much on my own?

Getting support isn't weakness, it's smart. We're not built to handle everything solo.

What soothes your nervous system?

Your nervous system is your body's stress detector. When it senses threat, even emotional or social stress, it gets stuck in *fight*, *flight*, or *freeze* mode. You feel wired, anxious, shut down, or exhausted.

Soothing it means reminding your body: You're safe now. You can exhale.

Here are a few ways to calm your system:
- Breathe deeply. Slow breathing tells your body to chill. Try four seconds in, four seconds out, for a few minutes.
- Move your body. A walk. Stretching. Dancing. Movement helps shake off stress hormones.
- Laugh. Even just smiling or watching something funny releases tension.
- Connect. Call a friend. Hug your pet. Human connection soothes your system faster than scrolling ever will.
- Ground yourself. Touch something real. Notice five things you can see, four you can feel, three you can hear... This pulls you out of stress spirals.

Stress isn't your enemy—it's your body trying to keep you safe. The key is learning when to push forward and when to step back, simplify, and soothe.

Task: Stress SOS & Esteem Builder

1. Stress SOS:
Write your top three stress triggers. Then list two things that calm you for each.

2. Self-Esteem Anchor:
Each night, write one thing you did that day you're proud of, even if it's small. You're building evidence of your strength.

SOCIAL MEDIA

It connects. It inspires. It also distorts. Likes aren't love. Followers aren't friendships. Filters aren't reality.

It's easy to confuse online attention with real connection, especially when it feels good in the moment. But love isn't measured in hearts, shares, or fire emojis. Friendship isn't someone watching your stories. And a perfect selfie doesn't mean a perfect life.

What you see online is a highlight reel, edited, filtered, and carefully chosen. Real connection is messier than that. It's honest. Unfiltered. Imperfect. You don't need a massive following to be worthy. You only need a few people who see the real you and stick around when the filters are off.

Social media was designed to keep your eyes glued to the screen, not to make you feel better about yourself. The endless scroll? That's no accident. Algorithms are built to feed you content that triggers emotion, especially outrage, comparison, or envy, because that's what keeps you scrolling.

And the more you scroll, the harder it gets to focus, think clearly, or just be content in your own life. Research shows that *heavy social media and AI-driven content consumption* can affect your brain's reward system. Too much screen time can reduce *dopamine sensitivity*, which means you need more stimulation to feel the same level of pleasure. It can also increase anxiety, make it harder to focus, and lower your ability to stay present in real life.

Even worse? Constantly relying on AI or quick answers instead of thinking through problems yourself can lead to *cognitive decline*—your brain stops practicing the very skills it needs to grow.

So how do you take back control?

Here are some simple but powerful tips:
- Don't compare your behind-the-scenes to someone else's highlight reel. You're seeing the best 5% of someone's life, not their real struggles.
- Unfollow accounts that trigger insecurity. If someone's content makes you feel anxious, unworthy, or less-than, let it go. You are allowed to protect your peace.
- Set screen time limits to protect your attention. Your focus is a superpower, don't give it away to an algorithm. Use built-in tools to remind you to log off and check back into real life.
- Post when you want to express, not impress. Not everything needs to be a performance. Share what matters to *you*, not what will get the most likes.

And remember: You are allowed to exist unposted and unfiltered. You don't need to prove anything to anyone. You're already enough—even when no one's watching.

Quote to Remember
"You are not your feed. You are not your likes. You are not your body, your past, or your doubts. You are enough." — Liam Mulhall

Task: Self-Esteem Builder & Social Reset

1. Self-Esteem Boost:
Write down three non-appearance-based things you love about yourself. Please keep it in your wallet or the Notes app.

2. Social Reset:
Mute or unfollow five accounts that make you feel small. Follow five that inspire, uplift, or reflect the *real* you.

T TRUST, TIME MANAGEMENT, TOXICITY

Story: The Friend Who Took Too Much

David gave and gave. Time. Energy. Forgiveness. But his "best mate" only showed up when he wanted something. After one big betrayal, David finally said, "No, I can't do this anymore."

Some friendships aren't balanced — and holding on only hurts more. Sometimes the kindest thing you can do, for them and for yourself, is walk away with your dignity intact.

Advice & Wisdom

TRUST

Trust is built in drops and lost in buckets.

It takes time—small moments of honesty, consistency, and care—to earn someone's trust. One kind word. One promise kept. One moment where you showed up when it mattered. That's the drop. Over time, those drops add up.

But it only takes one big lie, one betrayal, one broken boundary to empty the bucket. That's why trust is precious and why rebuilding it takes patience, humility, and a whole lot of work. So, guard your trust. Earn it slowly. And if you break it—own it, apologise, and start filling that bucket again… one drop at a time.

To build trust:
- Be consistent.
- Do what you say.
- Own your mistakes.

To rebuild it:
- Apologise without excuses—take responsibility for the impact, not just your intention. A real apology doesn't defend, it listens, acknowledges, and heals.
- Give time and space.
- Let your actions do the talking.

TIME MANAGEMENT

Your time is your life. *Protect it.* Every hour you spend is a piece of energy, attention, and potential you will not get back. Use it like it matters—because it does.

Tips:
- Plan your week ahead—but stay flexible.

Having a plan gives you structure and reduces stress. It helps you prioritise what matters instead of reacting to everything last minute.

But life isn't always predictable. Don't beat yourself up if plans shift—flexibility is part of the process. Think of your schedule like a guide, not a cage.

Break big goals into small chunks.

If something feels overwhelming, it probably needs to be broken down. Instead of "study for the exam," try "revise two chapters" or "make flashcards for science." Instead of "clean my room," go with "set a timer for ten minutes" or "start with the floor."

Small, clear steps turn procrastination into momentum. It's not about doing everything at once—it's about doing *something* now.

- Learn to say "no"—it's not rude, it's wise.

Every "yes" is also a "no" to something else—your time, energy, sleep, focus. Saying no doesn't make you selfish. It makes you self-aware. They say "'no' is a complete sentence." And they're right. You don't always need a reason or a long explanation.

Still, if guilt creeps in, remind yourself: Saying no to protect your peace is better than saying yes and resenting it later.

TOXICITY

You can love someone and still walk away. Toxic doesn't always mean someone is evil or dangerous. It just means the relationship takes more from you than it gives back.

But not every relationship is easy to label. Some people make you laugh, help you feel seen, or seem fun in the moment—but still leave you emotionally drained. You don't need a relationship to be *all bad* to know it's not good for you.

If it consistently costs your peace, self-worth, or sense of safety—that's a sign.

Red flags to watch for:

- Manipulation.

This is when someone twists the truth, your words, or your feelings to control you. It might look like: "I never said that—you're just too sensitive." "If you really cared about me, you'd do this for me."

You'll feel confused, second-guess yourself, or like you're constantly walking on eggshells. That's not love—it's control disguised as connection.

- Guilt trips.

Guilt trips are subtle emotional pressure. Instead of asking directly, the person makes you feel bad for having boundaries, saying no, or needing space. It might sound like: "Wow, I guess I just don't matter to you." "Everyone else would've said yes—but okay."

Healthy relationships respect your decisions, even when they're inconvenient.

- Constant drama.

Toxic dynamics often thrive on chaos. There's always a crisis, someone's always upset, and things that should be small blow up fast. You might feel like you're constantly fixing things, smoothing things over, or calming them down.

You're not their emotional firefighter—and you're not the problem if you want peace.

- One-sided effort.

You're always the one checking in, apologising first, making the plans, keeping the friendship going. But when you need something? Silence.

Relationships should be a two-way street—not a dead-end with you doing all the work.

So, what do you do if you spot these signs?
- Don't wait for it to get worse. Trust your gut.
- Set clear boundaries and hold them.
- Limit contact or take space if needed.

- Talk to someone safe, like a friend, teacher, or counsellor, and get a second perspective.
- You don't need to burn bridges, but you *are* allowed to quietly walk away from the ones that are burning *you*.

You deserve relationships that feel safe, steady, and real. Not perfect—just respectful. And sometimes, choosing peace means letting go.

Quote to Remember
"Trust is sacred. Time is gold. Protect both—even if it means walking away from what you once held close." — Liam Mulhall

Task: Trust Inventory & Time Audit

1. Trust Inventory:
List three people you fully trust. What qualities make them safe? Now ask: do I offer those qualities too?

2. Time Audit:
Track how you spent your last hours. What drained you? What filled you? Adjust accordingly.

U UNDERSTANDING, UNCERTAINTY, UNIQUENESS

Story: The Test Without Answers

Sophie always wanted certainty. She liked clear paths and straight answers. But she felt lost when life threw curveballs—a breakup, a university rejection, a family fight.

Until she stopped *fighting* the unknown and started *flowing* with it. Growth came not from control, but from surrender.

Advice & Wisdom

UNDERSTANDING

Most fights don't start with bad intentions, they start with misunderstandings.

Someone reads a message the wrong way. Someone assumes instead of asking. Someone feels unheard, unseen, or dismissed.

That's why understanding matters. And it starts with slowing down.

- Ask questions before making assumptions.

Not everything needs a reaction. Sometimes it needs clarification. "What did you mean by that?" "Hey, can I check if I heard that right?" A simple question can prevent a major fallout.

- Listen longer than you speak.

It's easy to talk over someone. It's harder—but more powerful—to *really* listen.

Listening doesn't mean agreeing. It means respecting others' opinions. It means trying to understand where they're coming from, not just waiting to respond.

- Be open to what you don't know.

You don't know everything someone's going through. They might be stressed, hurting, or just having a bad day. Staying open keeps you curious, not combative.

- Understanding doesn't mean you have to agree.

It just means you care enough to try—and that effort can change everything.

UNCERTAINTY

Life is uncertain—and weirdly, that's where the magic lives. If everything were predictable, nothing would grow. Uncertainty can feel scary, but it's also where possibility begins.

Tips for peace in uncertainty:
- Focus on what you *can* control.

You can't always control outcomes, but you *can* control how you show up: your actions, your attitude, your words. That's your power. Don't give it away.

- Trust that clarity comes with movement.

You won't always have the full map. But clarity rarely strikes while standing still. Take one step. Try something. Reach out. Show up.

Momentum creates insight—because experience teaches what overthinking can't.

- Embrace "not knowing" as part of becoming.

Not knowing isn't failure. It's *becoming*. It means you're learning, unfolding, becoming more you—and that takes time.

- You don't need all the answers to move forward.

Just enough courage to take the next step.

UNIQUENESS

Your quirks, your scars, your weirdness—they're not flaws. They're your fingerprint. Your story. The things that make you unforgettable.

You weren't born to blend in. You were born to shine through. It's easy to feel like you need to edit yourself to fit in—to be quieter, cooler, more "normal." But "normal" is just a moving target created by comparison, and comparison is a thief. It robs you of self-respect, confidence, and the joy of being real.

You don't need to be like everyone else to matter. In fact, the world needs your *difference*. Your unique view, your odd ideas, your bold questions. That's where creativity and courage live—in the parts of you that *don't* match the crowd.

Signs you're owning your uniqueness:

At first, you didn't even realise you were hiding yourself.
- You laughed when others laughed, even when it wasn't funny.
- You stayed quiet in conversations, afraid your real opinions might not be "cool" enough.
- You wore what helped you blend in, not what made you feel good.

- You avoided your weird quirks, creative ideas, or passions, just in case someone judged you.

But then something changed.

You started owning your uniqueness:
- You stopped shrinking your opinions just to keep the peace.
- You laughed loud when something *made* you laugh.
- You wore what made you feel like *you*, even if it wasn't trending.
- You began to like your own company, not because you're perfect, but because you finally see that you're enough.

Comparison says, "Be like them." Confidence says, "Be more *you*." So, ask yourself: "What makes me different—and can I *celebrate* that instead of hiding it?"

Quote to Remember

"You were never meant to fit the mould. You were made to shape the world." — Liam Mulhall

Task: Uncertainty List & Uniqueness Boost

1. What I Don't Know (Yet):
Write down five things you're unsure about. They can be big or small—your future, a friendship, a decision, your identity, your place in the world.

Next to each one, write: "And that's okay."

Now pause. Breathe. And let go—not of the *question* itself, but of the pressure to solve it right now. Let go of:
- The *need* to have every answer.
- The fear that if you don't figure it out immediately, something's wrong.
- The attachment to certainty.

Uncertainty isn't failure. It's the space where new things can grow. You don't have to rush through the unknown. Some of life's biggest answers only come when you stop trying to force them.

2. My Weird Wins:

List five things that make you different. Frame them as strengths.

V VIRGINITY, VIRTUES, VALUES

Story: The "First Time" Myth

At school, losing your virginity was treated like a trophy—something to win, fast. But deep down, Dylan knew he wasn't ready.

He didn't wait out of fear. He waited because he trusted himself. Because he knew what mattered most wasn't doing it early—it was doing it on his own terms.

When it finally happened, it felt right. No guilt. No pressure. Just something real—and no regrets.

Advice & Wisdom

VIRGINITY

It doesn't define your worth. It's not a race. It's your choice—when, why, and with whom.

Some people choose to wait. Others don't. Some never do. That's okay—because what matters most is that it's your decision, made from a place of honesty and care.

What really matters:
- Readiness.

You're ready when you feel emotionally and physically prepared, not confused, not pressured, and not trying to impress anyone. Ask yourself: "Would I still feel good about this tomorrow?" "Am I doing this for me, not someone else?" "Do I feel respected, safe, and in control?"

- Respect.

For yourself, and the other person. It's not about trying to earn love, fit in, or meet someone else's timeline. It's about checking in, emotionally and physically, and being honest about what you want and don't want.

- Communication.

A healthy choice around sex includes honest conversations about boundaries, protection, expectations, and feelings. No shame. No pressure. Just openness.

And most importantly: You don't owe anyone your body. You don't have to explain your "yes" or your "no." You don't need to follow anyone's timeline but your own.

VIRTUES & VALUES

These are your *inner compass*. They guide decisions when emotions run wild.

Examples:

- Honesty.
- Loyalty.
- Courage.
- Kindness.

If your actions go against your values, you'll feel it. That feeling might show up as guilt, anxiety, or just an uncomfortable weight in your chest.

It might sound like that inner voice saying, "This doesn't sit right with me," even if everyone else is doing it. You might feel restless, irritable, or strangely flat—like something's off, but you can't name it. That's your gut speaking.

It's not there to ruin your fun, it's trying to keep you aligned with who you really are. Learn to listen. When you ignore it too long, you lose your sense of self. But when you honour it? You feel more grounded, more confident, and more at peace with your choices—even the hard ones.

Quote to Remember
"Protect your body, guard your values, and don't trade either for temporary approval." — Liam Mulhall

Task: Value Sorter

From this list, choose five that matter most to you right now: Honesty, Loyalty, Growth, Adventure, Kindness, Strength, Peace, Faith, Creativity, Love.

Then, for each one, write down *one action* you'll take this week to live that value.

For example:
- *Kindness → I'll check in on a friend who's been quiet.*
- *Growth → I'll try something that scares me a little.*

You don't have to pick the same five every week. Your values can shift as you grow—so experiment, reflect, and find the ones that feel true to who you are becoming.

This is how you build a life that feels like yours.

W WORRY, WORK ETHIC, WORTHINESS

Story: The What-If Spiral

Taryn had always been afraid of getting things wrong. She kept quiet in class, avoided challenges, and pretended everything was okay even when it wasn't. But eventually, she asked herself something different: "What would happen if I stopped letting fear decide everything?"

She didn't suddenly become fearless—but she started trying anyway. She spoke up. She took small risks. And with every step, she noticed something important: fear didn't disappear, but it got smaller the more she moved through it.

Advice & Wisdom

WORRY

It's a thief. It steals your peace and gives you nothing in return.

When your thoughts start spiralling, try these tips:

- Breathe deeply and anchor yourself.

That means grounding your body and mind in the present moment. For example, you can try feeling your feet flat on the floor, naming five things you can see, four you can touch, three you can hear, holding something cool or textured, like a rock, ice cube, or piece of fabric.

These small acts pull your brain out of the future where worry lives and back into now.

- Focus on the next small step, not the whole staircase.

When everything feels too big, zoom in. What's one small action you can take today? Worry feeds on overwhelm. Action quiets it.

- Ask: "Will this matter in five days, five months, five years?"

Most of the things we stress about won't even cross our minds a week from now. Use this question to reset your perspective.

Worry doesn't disappear overnight. But when you stop feeding it, it gets smaller. Start with your breath, your body, your next step.

WORK ETHIC

"Work like it matters. Know that you matter, too."

Let's start with work ethic.

Michael Jordan wasn't the greatest basketball player of all time just because he was born with talent. He was the first in the gym and the last to leave. He had a fire that most players didn't. His work ethic was relentless. People remember the six championships, the highlights, the buzzer beaters, but it was not those moments that made him great.

It was the thousands of hours of sweat, focus, and discipline that no one saw.

He once said: "I've missed more than nine thousand shots in my career. I've lost almost three hundred games. Twenty-six times I've been trusted to take the game-winning shot and missed. I've failed over and over again in my life. And that is why I succeed."

You wouldn't even know his name if he didn't have the work ethic. He would've been just another NBA player. But he wasn't. He was the one who outworked everyone.

You don't need to be Michael Jordan to have a solid work ethic. Just be the kind of person who:
- Turns up even when they don't feel like it.
- Stays late to learn the things they didn't get.
- Does the extra rep, the extra page, the extra mile.

That's what separates ordinary from exceptional.

But here's the truth: All the hard work in the world means nothing if you don't believe you're worthy of the success it brings. Work ethic gets you to the door. Worthiness is what lets you walk through it.

You're allowed to succeed. You're allowed to feel proud. You don't have to shrink yourself for anyone. So, don't work hard to prove you're enough. Work hard because you already are.

And who knows, maybe one day someone will say your name like they say Michael Jordan's.

WORTHINESS

You don't have to earn the right to matter. You already do.

Here's something a lot of people never get told: You are allowed to be proud of yourself. You're allowed to succeed. You're allowed to be seen.

Sometimes we work ourselves into the ground thinking we have to prove we're good enough. But what if you believed you already are?

Your worth isn't tied to:
- Your test scores.
- Your social media followers.
- Whether your parents are proud.

You are enough just by being you. Hard work is great, but don't confuse it with earning love, respect, or value. You're worthy of kindness. Worthy of good things. It's worth getting back up after you fall.

So, when you show up and work hard, do it because you believe in yourself—not because you think you're flawed or need fixing.

You're growing into something strong and steady. And that journey? It matters just as much as the destination.

Quote to Remember
"You are worthy even when you doubt it. Especially then." — Liam Mulhall

Task: Worry Shrinker & Worthy Reminder

1. Write your biggest worry right now.
Now write: "Even if this happens, I will still be okay because…" Find your strength.

2. Worth List:
Write ten reasons you are worthy. Don't stop until you hit ten.

X X-FACTOR (YOUR UNIQUE GIFT)

Story: The Talent He Hid

Liam could draw like a pro, but never showed it to anyone because he didn't think it was "cool." One day, he drew something for a kid being bullied. That drawing made the kid feel seen. From that day, Liam never hid his gift again.

Advice & Wisdom

X-FACTOR (YOUR UNIQUE GIFT)

Your X-Factor is the unique energy, talent, or perspective that only *you* bring into the world.

It doesn't need a spotlight or a crowd to matter. It's about what makes you feel most alive, the thing that energises you and makes others feel inspired just by being around you.

You don't need to be loud or outgoing to have it. You don't need to be perfect or first place to develop it. What matters is getting curious about who you are, what excites you, and what comes naturally when you stop trying to be someone else.

Your X-Factor shows up when you express yourself honestly and with courage, even in small moments.

Comedian Jimmy Carr once said on a podcast that his life changed after reading a book called *What Colour Is Your Parachute?* which is a workbook that helps you determine what you're good at, what makes you tick. It helped him realise his X-Factor wasn't just humour but connection through storytelling. That book gave him clarity.

So maybe try reading it too. Or ask your friends and family; what do they see in you? The people who know you best often notice strengths you overlook.

Maybe your X-Factor is...
- Making people laugh when they need it most.
- Listening, like *really listening*.
- Thinking deeply.
- Leading with calm.
- Seeing patterns.
- Creating art, ideas, or space for others to shine.

Whatever it is, it matters. You don't need to fit into a mould to be valuable. You need to know your lane and run in it with heart.

Quote to Remember
"Your X-Factor doesn't need applause. Just expression."— Liam Mulhall

Task: X-Factor Spotlight
Ask three people: "What's something I'm good at?" Take their answers. Reflect. Then use your gift this week to help someone.

Y YES VS. NO, YOUTH POWER, YOU MATTER

Story: The First Time She Said No

Ava said "yes" too often, to friends, teachers, and pressure. One day, she said "no" to a party she didn't feel right about. She thought she'd lose friends. She didn't. She gained self-respect!

Advice & Wisdom

YES VS. NO

Saying "yes" when you really mean "no" chips away at your self-respect.

Your time, your body, your energy—they belong to *you*. It's okay to say "no" without over-explaining. It's also okay to say "yes" when it feels right.

Both words carry power. Use them with honesty and intention.

YOUTH POWER

You are not "just a kid." You're a force. A spark. A voice that matters more than you know. Throughout history, young people have sparked real change.

- Malala Yousafzai stood up for girls' right to education when she was just a teenager.

- Greta Thunberg launched a global climate movement by skipping school to protest.
- Students in the U.S. helped launch the civil rights movement with sit-ins and protests.
- Even in your own school or community, chances are someone your age has spoken up and made a difference.

Age doesn't limit your impact, silence does.

To own your voice means to speak honestly about what you care about. It means asking questions, sharing your ideas, standing up when something doesn't feel right, even if your voice shakes. It doesn't mean shouting the loudest. It means speaking from truth.

And it's needed more than ever. The world is full of problems, but it's also full of possibility. Your ideas, your creativity, your courage, they shape the future.

So don't wait for "someday." You don't need permission to care, to create, or to lead. Start now, right where you are. Because you're not "just" anything. You're already enough to start something big.

YOU MATTER

Read that again: You matter!

Not because of your grades. Not because you're popular. Not because you're perfect. You matter because you're here. That's enough.

We live in a world that tries to tell you otherwise, that your worth depends on how many followers you have, how well you perform, or how "together" you look on the outside. But the truth is that your value isn't up for debate. You're not a product. You're a person. A living, breathing, growing human being.

And that is enough. Even if you feel invisible. Even if you've made mistakes. Even if you're still figuring it all out.

You matter, especially when it doesn't feel like it. Those days aren't the end of your story; they're just a page. And even if it feels like no one notices, someone out there will miss you deeply if you were gone. Please believe that.

This world wouldn't be the same without you. Please stay in it. Someone, somewhere, is alive because you exist.

If there's one thing you take from this book, let it be this: You don't have to earn the right to be loved. You already are.

So stay. Keep showing up. Let your story unfold one messy, beautiful, honest page at a time.

Quote to Remember
"Say no without guilt. Say yes with passion. And never forget—you are irreplaceable." — Liam Mulhall

Task: Self-Permission Slip

Write this down: "I give myself permission to…" Now finish the sentence with three things that matter to you.

Some ideas:
- "I give myself permission to rest."
- "I give myself permission to speak up."
- "I give myself permission to say no."

Or come up with your own. What do you really need right now?

You don't need anyone else's approval to take care of yourself. Start by giving it to yourself.

Z ZEST FOR LIFE, ZERO REGRETS, ZONES (COMFORT VS GROWTH)

Story: The Leap

Jordan had the chance to move cities for an opportunity. It scared him and he almost said no. But something deep inside said, "Go."

He left. It was hard and uncomfortable, but it changed his life. He didn't play it safe. He lived with zest and zero regrets.

Advice & Wisdom

Zest

Live with fire. Love with all your heart. Laugh loudly. Dance badly. Show up fully.

Life's too short for "meh." Too short to spend every day half-asleep, half-interested, or half-showing up.

Zest is that spark, the energy you bring into the room, the enthusiasm in your voice, the courage to care even when others act too cool to try. It's not about being loud or dramatic. It's about being *alive* in what you do.

You don't need to fake it. You just need to *find it*. Find what lights you up and chase more of it. Find who makes you laugh and keep them close. Find the weird, fun, passionate parts of yourself and let them breathe.

Zest isn't about perfection. It's about being in the moment, even when it's messy. It's about *trying*, even when you might fail. It's about caring, even when others shrug.

Why it matters:
- Zest gives you energy, even on hard days.
- It helps you take risks, grow, and feel more alive.
- It makes life feel richer, realer, and more *you*.

So go all in. Laugh too hard. Cry if you need. Try things. Be curious. Be bold. Because your life isn't a rehearsal, it's the real deal.

And you deserve to live it with your whole heart.

ZERO REGRETS

Regret usually doesn't come from failing—it comes from *not trying at all*. Not sending the message. Not joining the team. Not taking the risk. It's the silence, not the stumble, that keeps people up at night.

Living with zero regrets doesn't mean saying yes to everything or acting without thinking. It means *living intentionally*. It means knowing your values, trusting your gut, and backing yourself even when it's scary.

What living with zero regrets looks like:
- Saying how you feel—even if your voice shakes.
- Taking a shot at something you care about—even if it doesn't work out.
- Walking away from what's wrong—even if it's hard.
- Trying, failing, learning—and *still* trying again.

It's not about being reckless. It's about being *real*.

There's a difference between chasing a moment and choosing what matters. One fades fast. The other shapes who you become. So, take the chance. Say the words. Show up with your whole heart. Even if it doesn't work out, you'll walk away knowing you had the courage to try.

And that's something no one can take from you.

ZONES (COMFORT VS GROWTH)

You've probably heard it before: *"Get out of your comfort zone."* But what does that mean?

Your comfort zone is the space where things feel familiar. You know what to expect, and there's little risk of failure or embarrassment. It's safe and that's not always a bad thing. Everyone needs comfort sometimes. But when comfort becomes your default, it can quietly hold you back from growing into the person you're meant to be.

Growth lives just beyond that comfort. Not miles away, just beyond. It shows up in *moments that feel awkward or intimidating:*
- Putting your hand up in class.
- Trying out for the team.
- Speaking up when you'd usually stay quiet.
- Doing something you've never done before.

Those moments feel scary *because* they matter.

The truth is, doing hard things builds real confidence. Confidence doesn't come from thinking you're good at something, it comes from *proving* to yourself that you can survive discomfort. You mess up, try again, improve, and slowly, the thing that once scared you becomes your new normal.

This isn't about chasing pain or pushing yourself to the point of burnout. It's about being honest with yourself: Are you staying comfortable because it's what's best for you? Or because it's easier in the moment?

Sometimes, the hardest part is starting. But that first step, even if it's shaky, begins to stretch your limits. And every time you stretch a little more, your world expands.

There's a quote from former Navy SEAL David Goggins: *"Be comfortable being uncomfortable."* It means you don't wait to feel brave, you act *while* feeling afraid. And in doing that, you build the kind of grit that lasts a lifetime.

Avoiding hard things might feel good today. But facing them? That's what changes your future.

So, next time something scares you, not because it's dangerous, but because it matters, pause. Breathe. And take the step anyway.

That's where the magic begins.

Quotes to Remember
"Play with fire, chase what matters, and dare to grow beyond what feels safe — that's how you build a life worth remembering." — Liam Mulhall

Task: Zest List & Zone Step

1. Zest List:
Write five things that make you feel alive. Do one this week.

2. Zone Step:
Write one thing outside your comfort zone and take a small step toward it.

CONGRATULATIONS, GRADUATE OF EARTH SCHOOL (SO FAR...)

Well, well, well... Look who stuck around. Either you're deeply committed to self-growth, or avoiding homework, chores, or your screaming group chat. Either way, I'm proud of you.

Most people don't make it this far in a book without many pictures, but you saw it through, and that says something!

Seriously, though, if you've made it this far, it means something. It means you've taken the time to think, reflect, maybe even question things you've believed in your whole life. That takes guts!

So here it is, your final lesson, the one I left until the end for a reason:

Be Your Authentic Self!

Yeah, yeah, you've heard it before. But I need you to feel it now. This isn't just a feel-good social media quote. It's one of the most profound truths you'll ever carry.

I didn't get it until I hit my forties. Until I started letting go of who I thought I had to be, for approval, popularity, and safety, and started becoming who I actually was. It cost me some people, but it gave me myself back!

And I learned this most valuable lesson from a book that shook me to my core and opened my eyes up. It's called *The Top Five Regrets of the Dying*, and it was written by Bronnie Ware, a palliative care nurse from Australia, who listened to people at the end of their lives.

Do you know what one of the biggest regrets was? *"I wish I'd had the courage to live a life true to myself, not the life others expected of me."*

That hit me hard. And maybe it hits you too. Because the truth is, people will come and go. Approval fades. But you are here to stay.

So, be the weird kid. Be the kind kid. Be the quiet one, the loud one, the different one. Be the real one. If you try to be someone else, you might get by... But if you try to be yourself, you might fly.

One Last Analogy for the Road!

Think of yourself like a seed. Put that seed in the wrong soil, surrounded by weeds, with barely any sunlight or water? It won't grow. It'll survive, but barely.

But give it the right conditions? A little care. A little space. Good soil, good people. Sunlight in the form of love. Water in the form of truth. Then? You thrive.

You were meant to bloom. So don't shrink. Don't fake it. Just grow.

Your Last Line, Your Forever Mantra:

"Be real. Be kind. Be resilient. Be the reason someone else dares to be themselves, too."

Thanks for walking through *Earth School* with me. Now go out and live the life that you were born to live. Not someone else's.

Stay wild. Stay grounded. And remember: the world needs the real you.

— Liam Mulhall

ABOUT THE AUTHOR

Liam Mulhall grew up in a loving home in Ipswich, Queensland, raised between two worlds after his parents separated. There was always love, but no manual. Like many kids of divorced parents, he often felt confused. When his dad left, questions followed: "Was I not good enough?" "What did I do wrong?" "Why didn't he stay?"

He was raised by a hardworking single mum who gave him everything she could. She stepped in as a parent at school sports and father-son days. He loved her deeply for it, but the truth is, it was never quite the same. He often watched other boys with their dads and quietly wondered how different life might've been if he had that kind of role model in his corner.

When Liam was eleven, his older brother—then sixteen—moved out, and just like that, Liam went from being a kid to being the one who had to grow up fast. His mum, who had just lost her marriage and her partner, often leaned on Liam like an adult, needing someone to help her make sense of it all. It wasn't her fault. It was survival. But those early years fast-tracked him through childhood, shaping him in both painful and powerful ways.

What the world didn't always see was the trauma he carried from his father's anger. There were times—far too many to count—when Liam was hit for things no child should ever be punished for. Innocent curiosity was met with pain instead of patience. He'd sneak into his dad's workshop to build things, mimic what he saw, trying to be like him. When things broke, as they do when kids try to make things, the punishment came swiftly and brutally. His mum would often shield him, even take the blame. He remembers hiding in corners, crying, only to hear her calmly tell his father she'd broken it or misplaced it. That kind of love is rare. That kind of mum is everything.

Around this time, Liam developed what he now calls "survival intuition," a sixth sense for tension, a radar that detected slammed doors and shifts in voice tone. If his dad was angry, Liam knew it, and he knew when to shut up, play small, or get away.

But despite the darkness, there were lights too. His best mate—still his mate—had a dad. A knockabout bloke, always up for a laugh, who took Liam fishing, camping, and treated him like one of his own. He was rough and rugged and had a heart of gold. He taught Liam little things, bloke things, and maybe unknowingly became the father figure Liam never had. It wasn't blood that made it matter. It was presence.

At school, Liam struggled. Undiagnosed ADHD and ADD meant he was either all in or nowhere at all. Teachers would say, "Liam is a bright student, but struggles to stay focused." And to be fair… they weren't wrong.

Liam's mind would drift into the clouds when he wasn't fully engaged. Not metaphorically, *literally*. He remembers staring out the window, completely captivated by the sky, when suddenly a familiar mosquito-like voice would cut in: "Mr. Mulhall… are you listening? Have you come back down to Earth yet?"

And like clockwork, he'd blink, look away from the clouds, and reply, "Yes, miss, I'm present" But mentally, he was still off somewhere, dreaming about life, or building things in his imagination that didn't involve math.

Then came the bullying. In Years 8 and 9, Liam was picked on and bullied. He never knew why. Maybe it was his smile, the one that masked the storm. But one summer, something changed. He decided he had

had enough. His older brother took him to buy a home gym, and Liam trained every day in their backyard shed for two months. No YouTube. No Google. No Instagram. Just an old *Encyclopedia Britannica* and sheer determination. He didn't have a dietitian, just steak and eggs, because someone once said it builds muscle. That was enough for him.

By Year 10, he had come back stronger. The bullying had stopped. He had found rugby league, his passion, and started carving a new path for himself.

Liam is of Wiradjuri descent, a proud part of his identity, even if he hasn't walked closely with language or tradition. He honours his heritage and the strength of his people with deep respect.

As an adult, Liam served as a military police K9 handler and later as a senior firefighter, two roles that pushed him into real-life situations where courage meant showing up even when you're scared. The military gave him structure when he could've easily gone off track. Firefighting gave him purpose. Among trauma and tragedy, he discovered the beauty in life's fragility and the power of showing up for others.

After getting medically retired from firefighting, Liam found a new path coaching young teenagers in rugby league, listening to their stories, feeling their struggles first-hand, and seeing how tough it can be to grow up in today's world. Inspired by their experiences and reflecting on his teenage years, he thought: "I wish I'd had a manual growing up." That was the spark and the driving force behind his writing a book like this.

His life has been far from easy, marked by mental health struggles, addiction, major surgeries, the pain of losing loved ones, and long stints in rehabilitation. He's made mistakes, played the victim, and learned the hard way. But through it all, he's kept showing up.

He wrote this book not as a teacher with a chalkboard, but as a fellow student at Earth School—someone who knows what it's like to feel invisible, confused, angry, and full of dreams that don't yet have shape. This book is for the kid staring out the window, hiding pain behind a smile, and wondering if they're good enough.

Well, you are!

Liam's message to young people is simple: Don't let your past define you. Don't let pain or poverty or pressure tell you who you are. And don't believe the lie that you're alone.

If you don't have a dad, find a mentor. If you don't feel safe at home, create your own "safe team." Your brain won't develop fully until you're twenty-five, so if you feel like a mess now, it doesn't mean you'll always be one. It just means you're still growing.

And with the right people around you? You'll grow into someone incredible.

Liam hopes this book becomes a compass. A quiet friend. A hand on your shoulder saying, "You've got this. Even if it's messy."

Because life isn't about perfection, it's about authenticity. And once you dare to be your authentic self, no matter who leaves or who stays, you'll finally be free.

After The Fire
Photo by Patrice Roblin Photography

CERTIFICATE OF COMPLETION

EARTH SCHOOL: A TEENAGER'S A TO Z GUIDE TO EMOTIONAL INTELLIGENCE

Presented to

_____

For successfully exploring the A to Z of life's greatest lessons with courage, reflection, and an open heart.

You've shown the emotional intelligence, resilience, and self-awareness it takes not just to survive — but to grow.

Awarded with gratitude and respect,

Liam Mulhall

Author, Mentor,
Fellow Student of Life

Date:

www.ingramcontent.com/pod-product-compliance
Lightning Source LLC
Chambersburg PA
CBHW020537080526
44583CB00013B/893